Microsoft® Office

Excel® 2007 Plain & Simple

Curtis Frye

PUBLISHED BY
Microsoft Press
A Division of Microsoft Corporation
One Microsoft Way
Redmond, Washington 98052-6399

Library of Congress Control Number: 2006937711

Printed and bound in the United States of America.

3 4 5 6 7 8 9   QWT   2 1 0 9

Distributed in Canada by H.B. Fenn and Company Ltd.

A CIP catalogue record for this book is available from the British Library.

Microsoft Press books are available through booksellers and distributors worldwide. For further information about international editions, contact your local Microsoft Corporation office or contact Microsoft Press International directly at fax (425) 936-7329. Visit our Web site at www.microsoft.com/mspress. Send comments to mspinput@microsoft.com.

Microsoft, Microsoft Press, Access, AutoSum, Calibri, Excel, Internet Explorer, PowerPoint, and Windows are either registered trademarks or trademarks of Microsoft Corporation in the United States and/or other countries. Other product and company names mentioned herein may be the trademarks of their respective owners.

The example companies, organizations, products, domain names, e-mail addresses, logos, people, places, and events depicted herein are fictitious. No association with any real company, organization, product, domain name, e-mail address, logo, person, place, or event is intended or should be inferred.

This book expresses the author's views and opinions. The information contained in this book is provided without any express, statutory, or implied warranties. Neither the authors, Microsoft Corporation, nor its resellers, or distributors will be held liable for any damages caused or alleged to be caused either directly or indirectly by this book.

Acquisitions Editor: Juliana Aldous Atkinson
Project Editor: Kathleen Atkins
Project Manager: Joell Smith-Borne of Abshier House
Compositor: Debbie Berman of Abshier House
Indexer: Kelly Dobbs Henthorne of Abshier House

Body Part No. X12-65198

To Virginia.

Contents

What do you think of this book? We want to hear from you!

Microsoft is interested in hearing your feedback so we can continually improve our books and learning resources for you. To participate in a brief online survey, please visit:

www.microsoft.com/learning/booksurvey/

v

4 Building a Workbook 31

5 Managing and Viewing Worksheets 57

6 Using Formulas and Functions 79

7 Formatting the Worksheet 99

8 Formatting the Worksheet 125

9 Printing Worksheets 143

10 Customizing Excel to the Way You Work 163

11 Sorting and Filtering Worksheet Data 179

12 Summarizing Data Visually Using Charts 195

13 Enhancing Your Worksheets with Graphics 213

14

Sharing Excel Data with Other Programs   233

15

Using Excel in a Group Environment   247

What do you think of this book? We want to hear from you!

Microsoft is interested in hearing your feedback so we can continually improve our books and learning resources for you. To participate in a brief online survey, please visit:

www.microsoft.com/learning/booksurvey/

Acknowledgments

I'm thrilled every time I get the chance to write a book for Microsoft Learning. Thanks go to Kathleen Atkins, Juliana Aldous-Atkinson, Sandra Haynes, and Lucinda Rowley for their support, trust, and faith in my efforts.

My sincere thanks also go out to Debbie Abshier, the principal of Abshier House, and Debbie Berman, Joell Smith-Borne, Kelly Dobbs Henthorne, Joyce Nielsen, and Beverly Scherf, all of whom turned my words into a book. It's a lot harder than it looks, and it takes a team of professionals who love what they're doing to make it happen.

Neil Salkind, my agent, represents both myself and Studio B with aplomb. He's represented me for ten years, and I'm continually amazed at how much he gets done every day.

I'd like to thank the folks of ComedySportz Portland, led by Pat Short. Improvisational comedy provides both an excellent preparation for and release from the pressures of writing.

Finally, I'd like to thank my family. My wife Virginia provides emotional support when I need it, demonstrates the work ethic of a former professional ballerina when I need it, and is always there when I need it. My brother Doug, father David, and mother Jane have all contributed to my success. Being able to write professionally, and make a good living doing it, means more to me than they'll ever know.

Introduction: About This Book

If you want to get the most from your computer and your software with the least amount of time and effort—and who doesn't?—this book is for you. You'll find *Microsoft Office Excel 2007 Plain & Simple* to be a straightforward, easy-to-read reference tool. With the premise that your computer should work for you, not you for it, this book's purpose is to help you get your work done quickly and efficiently so that you can get away from the computer and live your life.

No Computerese!

Let's face it—when there's a task you don't know how to do but you need to get it done in a hurry or when you're stuck in the middle of a task and can't figure out what to do next, there's nothing more frustrating than having to read page after page of technical background material. You want the information you need—nothing more, nothing less—and you want it now! It should be easy to find and understand.

That's what this book is all about. It's written in plain English—no jargon. There's no single task in the book that takes more than a couple pages. Just look up the task in the index or the table of contents, turn to the page, and there's the information you need, laid out in an illustrated step-by-step format. You don't get bogged down by the whys and wherefores: just follow the steps, and get your work done.

Occasionally, you might have to turn to another page if the procedure you're working on is accompanied by a "See Also." That's because a lot of tasks overlap, and I didn't want to keep repeating myself. I've scattered some useful tips here and there, and thrown in a "Try This" or a "Caution" once in a while, but by and large I've tried to remain true to the heart and soul of a "Plain & Simple" book, which is that the information you need should be available to you at a glance.

Useful Tasks...

Whether you use Excel 2007 at home or on the road, I've tried to pack this book with procedures for everything I could think of that you might want to do, from the simplest tasks to some of the more esoteric ones.

...And the Easiest Way to Do Them

Another thing I've tried to do in this book is find and document the easiest way to accomplish a task. Excel 2007 often provides a multitude of methods to accomplish a single end result—which can be daunting or delightful, depending on the way you like to work. If you tend to stick with one favorite and familiar approach, I think the methods described in this book are the way to go. If you like trying out alternative techniques, go ahead! The intuitiveness of Excel 2007 invites exploration, and you're likely to discover ways of doing things that you think are easier or that you like better than mine. If you do, great! It's exactly what the developers of Excel 2007 had in mind when they provided so many alternatives.

A Quick Overview

Your computer probably came with Excel 2007 preinstalled, but if you do have to install it yourself, Setup makes installation so simple that you won't need my help anyway. So, unlike many computer books, this one doesn't start with installation instructions and a list of system requirements.

Next, you don't have to read the sections of this book in any particular order. You can jump in, get the information you need, and then close the book and keep it near your computer until the next time you need to know how to get something done. But that doesn't mean I scattered the information about with wild abandon. I've organized the book so that the tasks you want to accomplish are arranged in two levels—you find the general type of task you're looking for under a main section title such as "Formatting the Worksheet," "Summarizing Data Visually Using Charts," "Using Excel in a Group Environment," and so on. Then, in each of those sections, the smaller tasks within the main task are arranged in a loose progression from the simplest to the more complex.

Section 1 introduces the book, while Section 2 fills you in on the most important new features of Excel 2007. The biggest difference between Excel 2007 and previous versions is that the menu and toolbar system has been replaced by a new user interface. Now, instead of having to look under a series of rocks to find the capability you want, you can find the command you want on the user interface ribbon and complete your task quickly. This section also describes how to format data based on its value, use data tables effectively, create more attractive charts, and save your workbooks in popular file formats.

Sections 3 and 4 cover the basics: starting Excel 2007 and shutting it down, sizing and arranging program windows, navigating in a workbook, using the user interface ribbon to have Excel do what you want it to do, and working with multiple

Excel documents at the same time. Section 3 also introduces galleries, which are collections of preset formats you can apply to worksheets, charts, and other Excel objects, and shows you how to get help from within Excel and on the Web. Section 4 contains a lot of useful information about entering text and data, including shortcuts you can use to enter an entire series of numbers or dates by typing values in just one or two cells. You'll also learn about using the Office Clipboard to manage items you cut and paste, running the spelling checker to ensure you haven't made any errors in your workbook, and finding and replacing text to update changes in customer addresses or product names.

Section 5 is all about managing and viewing worksheets—the "pages" of a workbook. In this section, you'll find out about selecting, renaming, moving, copying, inserting, and deleting worksheets, rows, columns, and cells. In Section 6, you'll get to know formulas and functions. You use formulas to calculate values, such as finding the sum of the values in a group of cells. Once you're up to speed on creating basic formulas, you'll learn how to save time by copying a formula from one cell and pasting it into as many other cells as you like. Finally, you'll extend your knowledge of formulas by creating powerful statements using the function library in Excel 2007.

Section 7 focuses on making your workbooks' cells look great. Here's where you'll learn techniques to make your data more readable, such as by changing font sizes and font colors, adding colors and shading to cells, and color-coding your sheet tabs to make them stand out. Section 8 describes similar techniques you can apply to your worksheets, such as moving, inserting, and deleting rows and columns, applying worksheet themes, and coloring sheet tabs to call attention to important information.

Section 9 is all about printing your Excel documents, whether that means printing all or just a portion of your

results. Your productivity should increase after reading Section 10, where you'll learn how to customize Excel 2007 for the way you work. I'll show you how to add commands to the Quick Access Toolbar, control which error messages appear, define rules Excel uses to replace oft-misspelled words, create workbooks from built-in templates, and create custom workbook templates you can use to create new workbooks based on those formats.

Section 11 is about sorting and filtering your data, techniques you can use to limit the data displayed in a worksheet and determine the order in which it is presented. Do you need to see all of the sales for a specific product but don't want to bother with the rest of the data for the moment? No problem.

A picture is worth ten thousand words (according to Confucius; the modern version of the saying shorts you by nine thousand words), and I'll show you how to use the new Excel 2007 charting engine to create and use charts to summarize your data visually in Section 12. In Section 13, you'll learn how to enhance your worksheets by adding graphics and pictures. You'll be surprised to learn just how easy it is to insert clip art, add a special text effect, or resize a photo you added to a worksheet.

Sections 14 and 15 are all about sharing the data in your Excel worksheets—whether it's with your colleagues, on the Internet, or with other programs. Section 14 shows you how to make Excel 2007 interact with other 2007 Microsoft Office system programs, such as by embedding documents from other programs into your Excel workbooks, exchanging data between Excel and Word, or importing a text file into an Excel worksheet. In Section 15, you'll learn how to use Excel in a group environment, to add comments to your worksheets, and to accept or reject the comments made by others. You'll also learn how to publish a worksheet to the Web as well as how to pull information from the Internet directly into your worksheets. This section also introduces the Extensible Markup Language (XML), a handy technology that enables you to exchange data among spreadsheet applications.

A Few Assumptions

I had to make a few educated guesses about you, my audience, when I started writing this book. Perhaps you just use Excel for personal reasons, tracking your household budget, doing some financial planning, or recording your times for weekend bike races. Maybe you run a small, home-based business, or you're an employee of a corporation where you use Excel to analyze and present sales or production data. Taking all these possibilities into account, I assumed you'd need to know how to create and work with Excel workbooks and worksheets, summarize your data in a variety of ways, format your documents so that they're easy to read, and then print the results or share them over the Web or distribute your data both ways.

Another assumption I made is that—initially, anyway— you'd use Excel 2007 just as it came, meaning that you'd be working with the standard user interface. I like the new user interface, so that's what I've described in the procedures and graphics throughout this book.

A Final Word (or Two)

I had three goals in writing this book:

- Whatever you want to do, I want the book to help you get it done.

- I want the book to help you discover how to do things you didn't know you wanted to do.

- And, finally, if I've achieved my first two goals, I'll be well on the way to the third, which is for my book to help you enjoy using Excel 2007. I think that's the best gift I could give you to thank you for buying my book.

I hope you'll have as much fun using *Microsoft Office Excel 2007 Plain & Simple* as I've had writing it. The best way to learn is by doing, and that's how I hope you'll use this book.

Jump right in!

What's New in Excel 2007?

One of the first things you'll notice about Microsoft Office Excel 2007 is that the user interface has changed quite a bit. Earlier versions of Excel had well over a thousand commands scattered among the program's menus and toolbars; what's more, some useful commands didn't appear on any of the menus or toolbars! In Excel 2007, you need to look in only one place for the tools you need to use Excel: the ribbon at the top of the program window. If you've used Excel before, you'll only need to spend a little bit of time working with the user interface to use the program skillfully. If you're new to Excel, you'll have a much easier time learning to use the program than you would have with the older user interface.

This section of the book introduces many of the new features in Excel 2007: the new user interface and especially the ribbon, the improved formatting capabilities provided by galleries and the Mini toolbar, the new capabilities offered by data tables, the new color management scheme, and the improved charting engine. You also have some new ways to manage the data in your workbooks. For example, you can tell Excel how to format your data based on its value, summarize your data by using new functions, and save your workbooks as documents in other useful file formats.

Touring the New User Interface

The most obvious change to the user interface is the ribbon, which replaces all the menus and toolbars you may be familiar with. After you've entered your data into a worksheet, you can change the data's appearance, summarize it, or sort it, using the commands on the ribbon. Unlike previous versions of Excel, which made you hunt through a complex toolbar and menu system to find the commands you wanted, everything you want to do can now be found in one place.

The ribbon divides its commands into seven tabs: Home, Insert, Page Layout, Formulas, Data, Review, and View. The following graphic shows the Home tab, which appears when you start Excel.

The Home tab contains a series of groups: Clipboard, Font, Alignment, Number, Styles, Cells, and Editing. Each group, in turn, hosts a series of controls that enable you to perform tasks related to that group (font formatting, cell alignment, number formats, and so on). Clicking a control with a downward-pointing arrow displays a menu or palette that contains further options; if an option has an ellipses (...) after the item's name, clicking the item displays a dialog box. You can also open a dialog box by clicking the Dialog Expander control at the bottom right corner of a group; that control looks like a square than contains an arrow pointing down and to the right.

Finally, you'll see the Microsoft Office button at the top left corner of the Excel program window. Clicking the Microsoft Office button enables you to save a workbook, create new workbooks, print a worksheet, change the Excel program options, and quit Excel.

Group   Dialog Expander

Arranging Data into Tables

You'll often discover that it makes sense to arrange your Excel data as a table, where each column contains a specific data element (such as an order number or the hours you worked on a given day) and each row contains data about a specific thing (such as the details of order number 1403). The following graphic shows an Excel 2007 data table.

In Excel 2007, tables make it easier for you to enter and summarize your data. If you want to add data to a table, just click in a cell in the row just below the table and type the data. Excel will recognize that you want the data to be part of the table and will expand to include it. You can also have Excel display a Totals row at the bottom of your table.

You have full control over your table's appearance and how it summarizes your data in the Totals row.

Table column header

Totals row

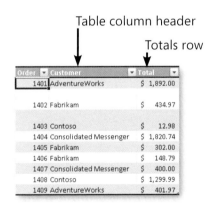

Introducing Galleries

In Excel 2007, you can apply formats to your Excel worksheets, charts, and other objects directly by selecting the appearance you want from a gallery. Excel 2007 has three types of galleries: the drop-down gallery, the grid layout gallery, and the embedded gallery. The following graphics show all three types of galleries.

Regardless of how Excel presents the gallery, you can format your object with one or two mouse clicks. You also have the ability to create custom gallery entries by clicking the New item at the bottom of some galleries and using the dialog box that appears to define your new gallery entry.

Grid layout

Drop-down

Embedded

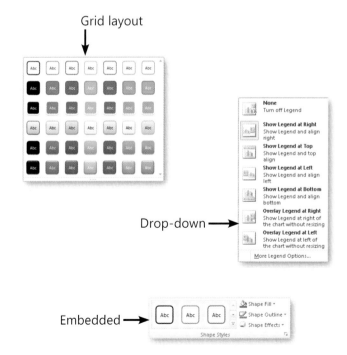

Using the Mini Toolbar

The Mini toolbar, which Microsoft interface designers originally called the "floatie," is a small formatting toolbar that appears at the top of the shortcut menu when you right-click something that can be formatted, such as a chart element or a selected group of cells. What's neat about the Mini toolbar is that it saves you several steps when you want to perform some simple formatting. Rather than having to go to the

ribbon, click the Home tab, find the formatting command you want, and then return to the ribbon tab that you need to use to manipulate your object, you can right-click the object and select your formatting quickly.

The graphic that follows shows the Mini toolbar at the top of a shortcut menu. And, yes, if you would prefer not to have the Mini toolbar appear, you can turn it off.

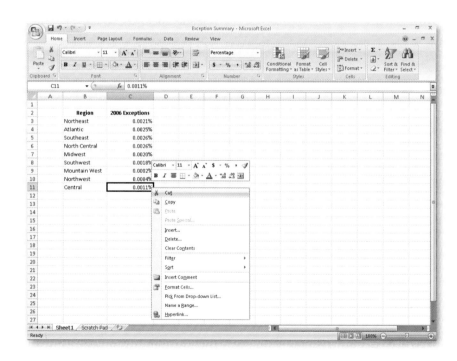

Creating Formulas Using New Functions

The Microsoft Excel programming team encourages users to suggest new capabilities that could be included in future versions of the program. Apparently, one of the most common requests from corporations using Excel was to find the average value of cells in which the value met certain criteria. For example, in a table listing orders, a formula could find the average amount of all orders over $1,000.

Here are quick descriptions of the new functions and any existing functions to which they're related. The following figure shows these functions in action, and lists the exact formula used to calculate the cell's values:

■ AVERAGEIF, which lets you find the average value of cells in a range for cells that meet a single criterion

■ AVERAGEIFS, which enables you to find the average value of cells in a range for cells that meet multiple criteria

■ SUMIFS, an extension of the SUMIF function, which enables you to find the sum of cells in a range for cells that meet multiple criteria

■ COUNTIFS, an extension of the COUNTIF function, which enables you to count the number of cells in a range that meet multiple criteria

■ IFERROR, an extension of the IF function, which lets you tell Excel what to do in case a cell's formula generates an error (as well as what to do if the formula works as expected)

Tip

Don't worry if you don't fully understand what these new functions do; you'll learn more about them later in this book.

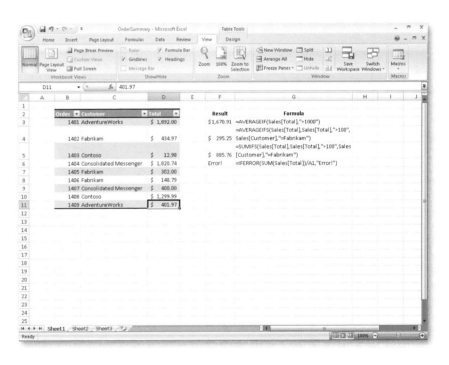

Using More Colors

Excel has always been a great program for analyzing numerical data, but even Excel 2003 came up a bit short in the presentation department. In Excel 2003 and earlier versions, you could have a maximum of 56 different colors in your workbook. In addition, you had no easy way to ensure that your colors looked good next to the other colors in your workbook; that is, unless you were a graphic designer and knew what you wanted going in.

Excel 2007 offers vast improvements over the color management and formatting options found in previous versions of the program. You can have as many different colors in a workbook as you like, for example, and you can assign a design theme to a workbook. Assigning a theme to a workbook offers you color choices that are part of a complementary whole, not just a dialog box with no guidance about which colors to choose.

The following graphic shows the range of themes from which you can choose and the colors available within one of those themes. And remember, you can pick any color you like; you're not limited to colors presented as part of a theme!

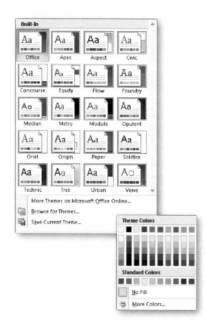

Creating Better Conditional Formats

Businesses often use Excel to track corporate spending and revenue. The actual figures are very important, of course, but it's also useful for managers to be able to glance at their data and determine whether the data exceeds expectations, falls within an acceptable range, or requires attention because the value falls below expectations. In versions prior to Excel 2007, you could create up to three conditions and define a format for each one. For example, you could create the following rules:

■ If monthly sales are more than 10 percent ahead of sales during the same month in the previous year, display the value in green;

■ If monthly sales are greater than or equal to sales during the same month in the previous year, but are less than 10 percent greater, display the value in yellow;

■ If monthly sales are less than sales during the same month in the previous year, display the value in red.

In Excel 2007 you can have as many rules as you like, apply several rules to a single data value, choose to stop evaluating rules after a particular rule has been applied, and change the order in which the rules are evaluated without having to delete and re-create the rules you change. As shown in the

figure, you can also apply several new types of conditional data formats: data bars, which create a horizontal bar across a cell indicating how large the value is; color gradients, which change a cell's fill color to indicate how large the value is; and icon sets, which display one of the available icons depending on the guidelines you establish.

Creating More Attractive Charts

Excel enables you to manage large amounts of numerical data effectively, but humans generally have a hard time determining patterns from that data if all they have to look at are the raw numbers. That's where charts come in. Charts summarize your data visually, which means that you and other decision-makers can quickly detect trends, determine high and low data points, and forecast future prospects using mathematical tools.

Excel 2007 marks a tremendous step forward in how Excel enables you to create attractive and informative charts quickly.

By using a set of special tabs on the ribbon just for charts, you can select the type of chart you want to create, how you want the chart formatted, and how you want specific elements to be laid out. Excel 2007 also takes advantage of the new 2007 Microsoft Office system graphic and drawing capabilities, enabling you to create professionally formatted charts in just a few steps. The following graphic shows just one chart that you can make with Excel.

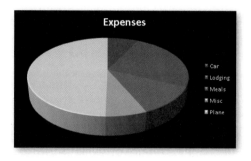

3 Getting Started with Excel 2007

Microsoft Excel 2007 is designed to help you store, summarize, and present data relevant to your business or home life. You can create spreadsheets to track products and sales, or, just as easily, build spreadsheets to keep track of your personal investments or your kids' soccer scores. Regardless of the specific use you have in mind, Excel is a versatile program you can use to store and retrieve data quickly.

Working with Excel is pretty straightforward. The program has a number of preconstructed workbooks you can use for tasks such as tracking work hours for you and your colleagues or computing loan payments, but you also have the freedom to create and format workbooks from scratch, giving you the flexibility to build any workbook you need.

This section of the book covers the basics: how to start Excel and shut it down, how to open Excel documents, how to change the Excel window's size and appearance, and how to get help from within the program. There's also an overview of the Excel window, with labels for the most important parts of the program, and a close-up look at the new user interface. You can use those images as touchstones for learning more about Excel.

Surveying the Excel Screen

In many ways, an Excel worksheet is like the ledger in your checkbook. The page is divided into rows and columns, and you can organize your data using those natural divisions as a guide. The box formed by the intersection of a row and a column is called a cell. You can identify individual cells by their column letters and row numbers—this combination, which identifies the first cell in the first column as cell A1, is called a cell reference. The following graphic shows you the important features of the Excel 2007 screen.

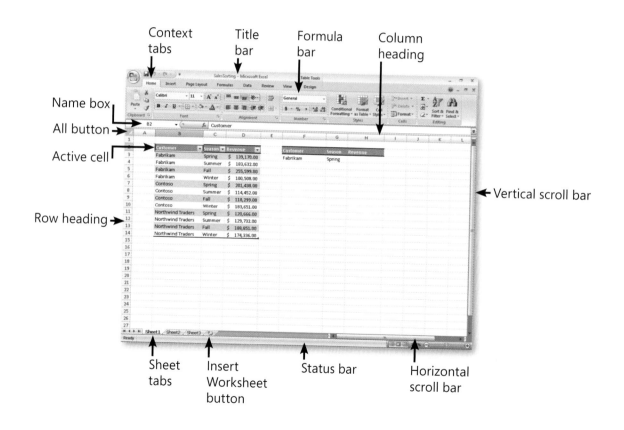

Working with the User Interface

When the Microsoft Office user interface design team sat down to update the 2007 Microsoft Office system, their goal was to give users a single place to look for commands. In previous versions of Office, you had to look through dozens of toolbars and menus to find specific commands. In Excel 2007, you can find what you need in one place: the ribbon at the top of the screen.

See Also

For more information on the user interface, see "Touring the New User Interface" on page 6.

Working with Galleries

After you've entered your data into a worksheet, you can change the data's appearance by using galleries that appear on the user interface. The ribbon has three types of galleries: galleries that appear in a dialog box, galleries that appear as a drop-down menu when you click a user interface item, and galleries that appear within the user interface itself. The following graphic shows a styles gallery and points out the gallery's controls.

One significant difference between Excel 2007 and previous versions of the program is how Excel tells you what will happen if you apply a formatting change. Rather than make you apply the change or click a preview button, Excel 2007 reformats the selected objects using the gallery item under your mouse pointer. All you need to do is move your mouse to see what your objects will look like when you're finished.

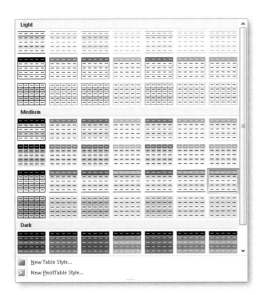

See Also

For a view of the three types of galleries in Excel 2007, see "Introducing Galleries" on page 7.

Starting Excel

After you've installed Excel on your computer, you can start it from the Start menu, which will open the program with a new, blank workbook, or by double-clicking an already existing Excel file on your computer.

Start Excel with a Blank Workbook

① Click the Start button on the taskbar.

② Point to All Programs.

③ Click Microsoft Office.

④ Click Microsoft Office Excel 2007.

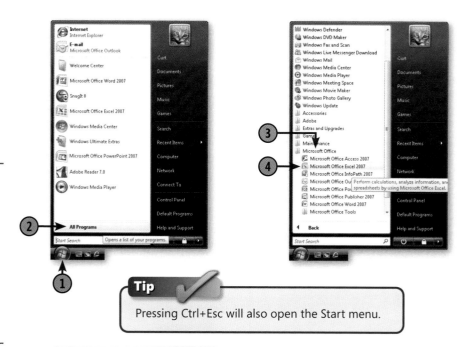

Tip

Pressing Ctrl+Esc will also open the Start menu.

Open an Existing Workbook

① Click the Start button on the taskbar.

② Click Computer.

③ Navigate to the folder that contains the file you want to open.

④ Double-click the file you want to open.

Tip

The Recent Documents menu, which you can display by clicking the Start button and pointing to Documents, lists recently used files. When you click an Excel file in the Recent Documents list, Excel will start and open the file.

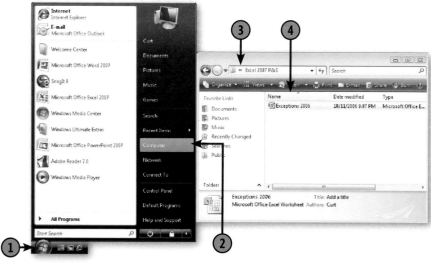

Finding and Opening Existing Workbooks

After you've created an Excel workbook, you will probably want to open it again, whether to verify the contents, add or update data, or copy data from one workbook to another. If you don't know the exact name of the file you want to open, but do know some of the data it contains, you can search for the file and open it after you've located it.

Open a Workbook

① Click the Microsoft Office button.

② Click Open.

③ Navigate to the folder that contains the workbook you want to open.

④ Click the workbook.

⑤ Click Open.

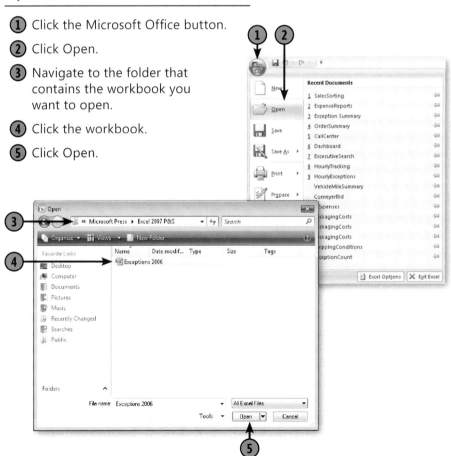

Open a Recently Used Workbook

① Click the Microsoft Office button.

② Click the workbook you want to open.

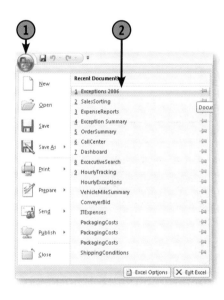

Search for a Workbook and Open It

① Click the Start button on the taskbar.

② Click Search.

③ Click Document.

④ Click the Advanced Search button.

⑤ Type all or part of the name of the workbook you want to find.

⑥ Type a word or phrase in the document.

⑦ Select the locations you want to search.

⑧ Click a file name in the Search Results list to open the file.

Tip

If your computer has several large hard disks, you should be sure to limit the locations you search by selecting only the hard disk where the file is most likely to reside. If you don't find the file in the first search, you can broaden your scope the next time.

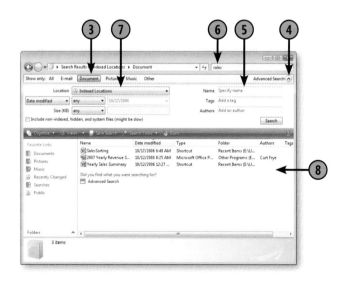

Using File Properties

Finding files can be difficult on computers you share with your colleagues or if you've been using the same computer for a long time and have created a lot of workbooks. You can make it easier to find your files by describing them in the Proper-ties. If you enter a term in a Properties field, you will be able to search using that term, even if it doesn't occur within the body of the workbook.

Set File Properties

① Open the file to which you want to assign property values.

② Click the Microsoft Office button.

③ Point to Prepare.

④ Click Properties.

⑤ Add information describing your file.

Tip

Adding words to the Keywords field is a great way to improve search results. Just type a word, press the space bar, and then type the next word. There's no need to use commas.

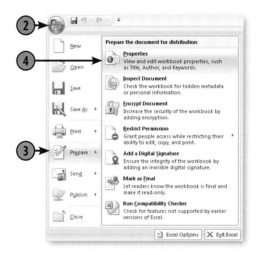

Define Custom Properties

1. Open the file for which you want to assign property values.

2. Click the Microsoft Office button.

3. Point to Prepare.

4. Click Properties.

5. Click the Document Properties down arrow.

6. Click Advanced Properties.

7. Click the Custom tab.

8. Select a property name.

9. Select the type of data contained in the property.

10. Type a value for the property.

11. Click Add.

12. Click OK.

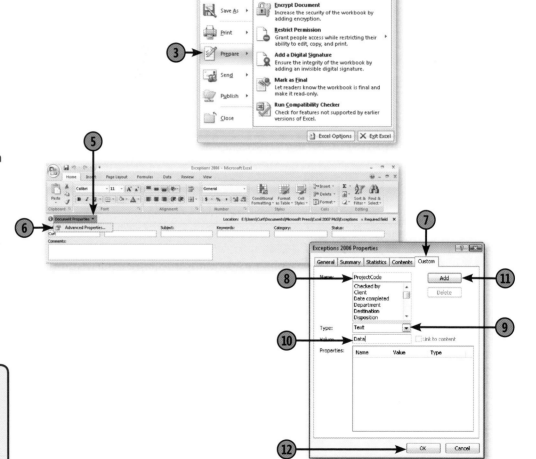

Creating a New Workbook

As a general rule, you should create a new workbook any time you need a place to store data on a new subject. For example, you might track your company's sales in one workbook, the products your company offers in another, and your employees' personal information and salaries in another.

Create a New Workbook

1 Click the Microsoft Office button.

2 Click New.

3 Click Blank Workbook.

4 Click Create.

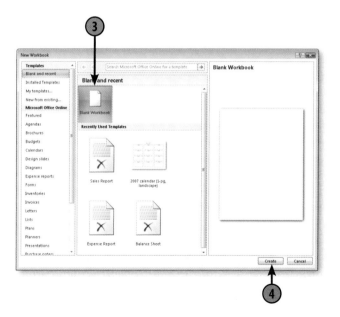

Working with Multiple Workbooks

When you create an Excel workbook for each subject of your business, you will sometimes need to look at data from more than one workbook to make your decisions. In cases like this, you can switch between them by choosing the workbook's name from the list displayed when you click the Switch Windows button on the View tab, or you can choose one of several arrangements so that you can work with your workbooks effectively.

Switch between Open Workbooks

① Click the View tab.

② Click Switch Windows.

③ Click the name of the workbook you want to display.

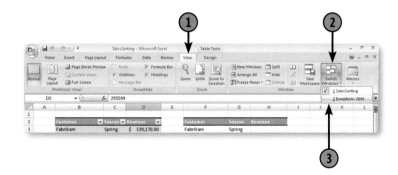

Show More than One Workbook

① Click the View tab.

② Click Arrange All.

③ Select the arrangement you want.

④ Click OK.

Try This!

Open three workbooks; then, on the View tab in the Window group, click Arrange All. In the Arrange All dialog box, select the Cascade option and click OK. The workbooks will be displayed with a slight overlap, with the full contents of the first workbook displayed and the title bars of the other two workbooks visible behind the first workbook.

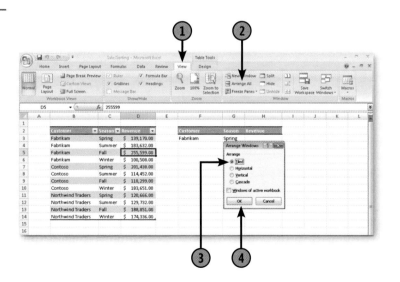

Sizing and Viewing Windows

You work with windows in the Excel program the same way you work with windows on your desktop. You can make a workbook's window as large as the screen itself; if you have more than one workbook open at a time, you can choose from several display arrangements to order the windows most effectively.

Resize a Window

- Click the Maximize button to make the window take up the entire screen.

- Click the Minimize button to represent the window as a button on the taskbar.

- Click the Restore button to return the window to its previous size.

- Drag the left or right border of the window to resize it horizontally.

- Drag the top or bottom border of the window to resize it vertically.

- Drag a corner to resize the window both horizontally and vertically.

- Drag the window's Title Bar to change its position.

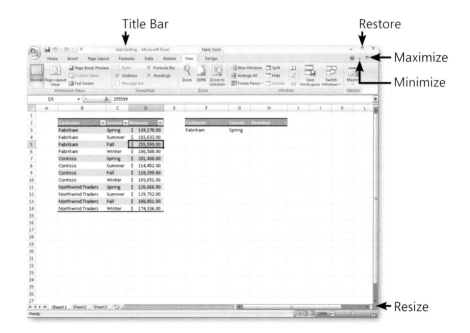

Title Bar

Restore

Maximize

Minimize

Resize

Tip

The Maximize and Restore buttons are actually two states of the same "window size" button, so you'll never see them on a window at the same time.

Zooming In or Out on a Worksheet

If you are not satisfied with how much of your worksheet you can see, you can make the worksheet larger or smaller without changing the window size. When you zoom out on a work-sheet, you can see the overall layout, but it might be difficult to read the data in individual cells. To get a better look at the data in your cells, you can zoom in on your worksheet.

Zoom In or Out

- Click the Zoom In control to make your window's contents 10 percent larger per click.

- Click the Zoom Out control to make your window's contents 10 percent smaller per click.

- Drag the Zoom slider control, shown in the figure, to the left to zoom out, or to the right to zoom in.

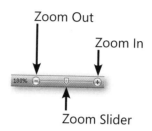

Zoom Out

Zoom In

Zoom Slider

Zoom In or Out to a Custom Zoom Level

1. Click the View tab.
2. Click Zoom.
3. Select the Custom option.
4. Type a new zoom level in the Custom field.
5. Click OK.

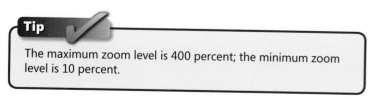

Tip

The maximum zoom level is 400 percent; the minimum zoom level is 10 percent.

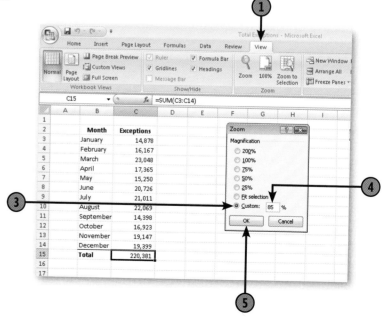

Viewing a Worksheet in Full Screen Mode

Occasionally, you'll want to see as much of a worksheet as possible. An easy way to temporarily hide the user interface ribbons at the top of the Excel window and the Status Bar at the bottom is to display the workbook in Full Screen mode. Unlike the Maximize command, which only affects one worksheet, in Full Screen mode you can view multiple worksheets simultaneously. If you want to format or otherwise manipulate the contents of your worksheet, you can select the cells and either hover over them to display the Mini toolbar or right-click a cell or object to display a shortcut menu.

You'll find the Close Full Screen command at the bottom of the shortcut menu that appears when you click a cell.

Turn Full Screen Mode On

① Click the View tab.

② Click Full Screen.

Turn Full Screen Mode Off

① Right-click a worksheet cell.

② Choose Close Full Screen.

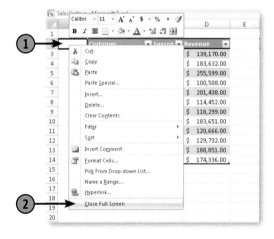

Saving and Closing an Excel Workbook

There's nothing more frustrating than losing a few minutes or even hours of work because you forgot to save your file. When you close your workbook, Excel checks to see whether it has changed since the last time you saved it. If it hasn't been saved, you'll be asked whether you want to save your workbook before you close it. If you want to save multiple versions of the same workbook, you can also create a copy of your file by saving it with a different name. Also, if you usually open workbooks that are saved in folders other than My Documents, you can change the folder that Excel displays by default in the Open and Save As dialog boxes.

Save a Workbook

1. Click the Save button on the Quick Access Toolbar.

Save a Workbook with a New Name

1. Click the Microsoft Office button.

2. Click Save As.

3. Navigate to the directory where you want to save your file.

4. Type the new file name.

5. Click Save.

Tip

A good rule of thumb is to save your workbook every time you make a change you would hate to have to make again.

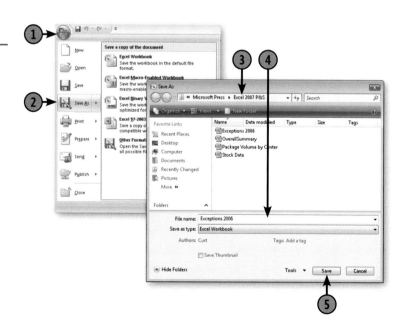

Change the Default File Folder

① Click the Microsoft Office button.

② Click Excel Options.

③ Click Save.

④ In the Default File Location field, type the path of the folder you want to appear by default.

⑤ Click OK.

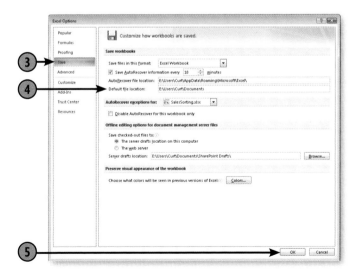

Close a Workbook

① Click the Microsoft Office button.

② Click Close.

③ If a dialog box appears asking whether you want to save any unsaved changes, you can do any of the following:

- Click Yes to save the workbook to the same name and location.

- Click No to discard all of the changes since the workbook was last saved.

- Click Cancel to return to the workbook.

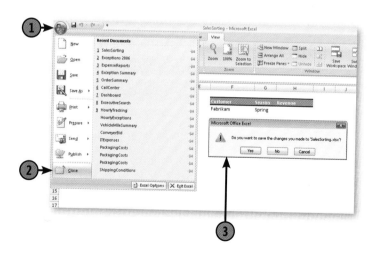

Exit Excel

① Click the Microsoft Office button.

② Click Exit Excel.

Caution

Make sure that you click the proper Close box. If you click the Close box at the top right of the Excel window, you'll close Excel, as well as the document on which you're working.

Using the Excel Help System

If you need to get help using Excel, you can look in a number of places. One option is to right-click an object (such as a worksheet or a graphic) to see a list of things you can do with the object. You can also open the Excel Help files and browse through them to find the answer to a specific question or just to explore.

Get Microsoft Excel Help

- Click the Microsoft Excel Help button.

Help button

Get Suggested Commands from Shortcut Menus

① Right-click any Excel object to see the shortcut menu of commands.

② Click a command.

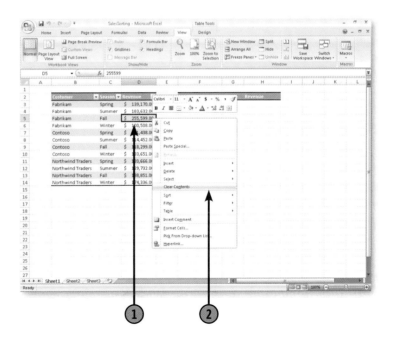

Get Help on the Web

① Click the Microsoft Office Excel Help button.

② Type your search terms.

③ Click the Search button.

④ Browse the topics displayed for help and resources.

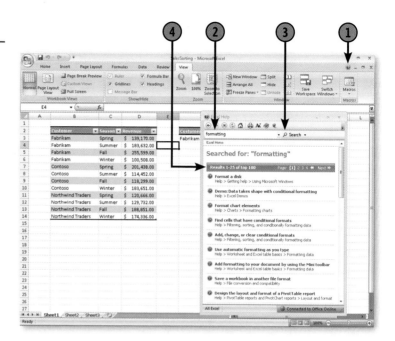

Tip

You can visit the Microsoft Office Assistance Center site directly by opening your Web browser and typing http://office.microsoft.com/assistance/ in the Address box.

4

Building a Workbook

One of the real strengths of Microsoft Excel is that the program makes it easy for you to enter large quantities of data with ease. When you type text, Excel remembers what you've entered in previous cells in the same column and offers to complete the current entry for you. The good news is that you'll only need to type "Arkadelphia" once. After the first time, typing the first three letters gives Excel enough information to guess the city name. Entering a series of numbers, dates, or days also goes quickly and smoothly. If you want to enter a long series of numbers, dates, or even weekdays, you can type one or two values and have Excel fill in the remaining values in the series! These techniques, combined with formatting and other skills you'll encounter elsewhere in this book, make data entry nearly painless.

Understanding How Excel Interprets Data Entry

Excel makes it easy for you to enter data into a worksheet by guessing the type of data you're entering and applying the appropriate formatting to that data. It's important to remember that because Excel is a computer program, it has some limitations. For example, Excel performs calculations using decimal values, such as .5, rather than using fractions, such as ½; however, if you do want to express some of your data as fractions and not as decimal values, you can do so by changing the cell's format to Fraction. In either case, you will be able to save the data in your preferred format.

Another aspect of this bias toward decimal values is that entering dates and times is much easier than it would be if you had to type out a full date, such as February 3, 2007. For example, if you type 2/3 in a cell and press Enter,

Excel will recognize the text as an abbreviation for the third day of the month of February and will display the data as 3-Feb.

You can choose the format you want for dates and times by selecting the cells that will hold dates or times, clicking the Home tab on the ribbon, and then clicking the Font dialog box launcher to display the Format Cells dialog box. Inside the dialog box, click the Number tab and then click Date in the list of categories. The available date formats will appear on the right. From there, just click the format you want and click OK. If you want the data in a cell to appear as a fraction, click the Number tab, click the Fraction category, specify the type of fraction on the right, and click OK. The following figure shows the Number tab with the Fraction category selected.

Navigating the Worksheet

Using the mouse and keyboard, you can move from cell to cell in a worksheet, move up or down a page at a time, or move to the first or last cell in a row. The following table lists the keyboard shortcuts you can use in addition to the scroll bars and sheet tabs you use with your mouse.

Navigate Your Workbook Using the Keyboard

Key	Action
Left Arrow	Move one cell left.
Right Arrow	Move one cell right.
Up Arrow	Move one cell up.
Down Arrow	Move one cell down.
Enter	Move one cell down.
Tab	Move one cell to the right.
Ctrl + Home	Move to cell A1.
Ctrl + End	Move to the last used cell in the worksheet.
Page Up	Move up one page.
Page Down	Move down one page.
Ctrl + Arrow Key	Move to the next cell with data in the direction of the arrow key. If there is not another cell in that direction, you move to the last cell in the worksheet in that direction.

Selecting Cells

Whenever you make changes to the cells in a worksheet, you can save time by applying the changes to similar cells at the same time. You used to be limited to selecting cells that were contiguous, but in Excel 2007 you can select groups of cells that aren't even next to each other! If your worksheet stores dates in cells with other information in between, you can select all of the date cells and apply a format to them at the same time.

Select a Contiguous Group of Cells

- Drag from the upper left cell you want to select to the lower right cell.

	Day					
VehicleID	Monday	Tuesday	Wednesday	Thursday	Friday	Saturday
V101	159	144	124	108	125	165
V102	113	106	111	116	119	97
V103	87	154	124	128	111	100
V104	137	100	158	96	127	158
V105	86	132	154	97	154	165
V106	159	163	155	101	89	160
V107	111	165	155	92	91	94
V108	101	162	123	87	93	140
V109	164	159	116	97	149	120
V110	100	107	143	144	152	132

Select a Noncontiguous Group of Cells

① Drag from the upper left cell you want to select to the lower right cell to select the first set of cells.

② Hold down the Ctrl key and drag from the upper left cell in another set of cells that you want to select to the lower right cell.

Select Rows or Columns

■ Drag from the first row or column header to the last row or column header you want to select.

Select Noncontiguous Rows or Columns

■ Hold down the Ctrl key, and then click the headers of the rows or columns you want to select.

Tip ✓

To deselect a selected group of cells, rows, or columns, click any cell in the worksheet.

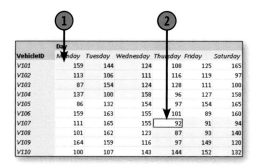

Column header

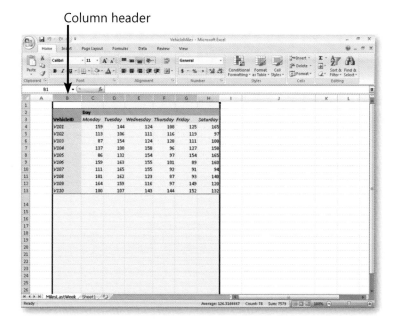

Entering Text in Cells

No workbook worthy of the name stays empty for long. You can type any sort of text you want directly into a cell, whether the text is a label identifying the data in a row or column or an explanation reminding you and your colleagues of any limitations on the data to be entered into a cell. Most text entered into Excel workbooks is short enough to fit on one line, but if you want to have the text in a cell appear on two or more lines and break at a specific location, you can easily insert a line break.

Enter Text as One Line

1. Click the cell into which you want to enter text.

2. Type the text you want to appear.

3. Press Enter.

See Also

For information about how to make your columns wider to allow more text to appear within a cell, see "Resize a Column" on page 132.

Enter Text with Forced Line Breaks

1. Click the cell into which you want to enter text.

2. Type the text you want to appear on the first line. Press Alt+Enter to insert a line break.

3. Type the text you want to appear on the second line, and then press Enter.

Try This!

Type a long line of text into a cell that is on an empty row. The text in this cell will extend over the other columns. Click the cell to the right of the one you just entered text into, type some text into it, and press Enter. The overlapping text in the previous column will be hidden.

Tip

In Excel 2007, the Formula Bar doesn't expand to display all of the information in a cell. To scroll through the contents of the Formula Bar one line at a time, use the scroll buttons at the right edge of the Formula Bar. To display the Formula Bar's entire contents, click the Expand Formula Bar control to the right of the Formula Bar. When you expand the Formula Bar, the Expand Formula Bar control changes to the Collapse Formula Bar control; clicking it returns the Formula Bar to its original one-line height.

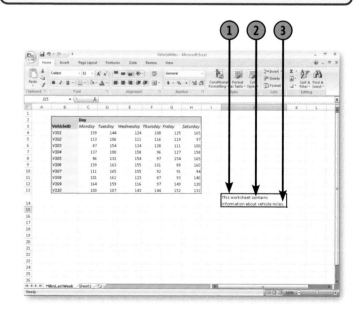

Entering Numbers in Cells

The backbone of any workbook is the numerical data in its worksheets, whether that data reflects sales, employee salaries, or the quantity of a given product you have in inventory. Entering numbers in Excel is as simple as clicking the cell and typing, but you can also enter very large or very small numbers using scientific notation. In scientific notation, a number with a positive exponent is written as 1.00E+06, which is read as "one times ten to the sixth power." Numbers that are less than one can be written with negative exponents. For example, the number .001 would be written as 1.00E-03 and read as "one times ten to the negative third power."

Enter Numbers

1. Click the cell into which you want to enter a number.

2. Type a numerical value.

3. Press Enter.

Enter Numbers Using Scientific Notation and Exponents

1. Click the cell into which you want to enter a number.

2. Type the base number you want.

3. Type E.

4. Type the exponent you want.

5. Press Enter.

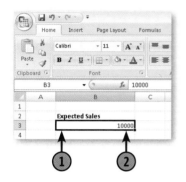

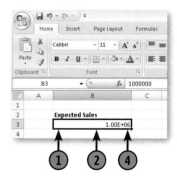

See Also

For information about applying number formatting such as dollar and percent signs instead of typing them, see "Formatting Cells Containing Numbers" on page 102.

Tip

You can type a number but have it interpreted as a text value by typing ' (an apostrophe) before the number value. The apostrophe will not appear in the cell, but a green icon will appear in the corner of the cell; clicking the cell exposes formatting options you can apply to the data.

Entering Dates and Times in Cells

Dates are extremely important in any business or personal situation, so Excel takes care to get them right. Excel understands dates no matter how you type them, so feel free to type them as needed. You can always change the formatting later.

Enter a Date

① Click the cell into which you want to enter a date.

② Type the month, day, and year, with each number separated by a slash (/) or a hyphen (-).

③ Press Enter.

Enter a Time

① Click the cell into which you want to enter a time.

② Type the hour, a colon (:), and the minutes. Press the space bar and type a or p for A.M. or P.M.

③ Press Enter.

Enter a Date and Time

① Click the cell into which you want to enter a date and time.

② Type a date, press the space bar, and then type a time.

③ Press Enter.

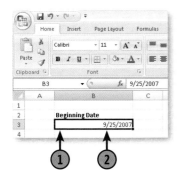

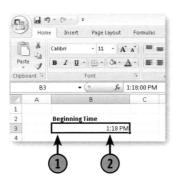

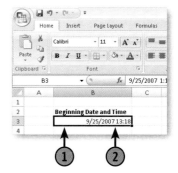

Caution

Different countries have different customs for writing dates. For example, 07/04/08 could mean July 4, 2008, or April 7, 2008, depending on where you live.

Enter the Current Date and Time

1 Click the cell into which you want to enter the current date and time.

2 Type =NOW()

3 Press Enter.

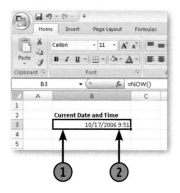

See Also

For more information about formatting cells with dates, see "Formatting Cells Containing Dates" on page 104.

Entering Data Using Fills

Entering long series of data, such as days in the month, weekdays, or a series of numbers with a definite progression, is tedious. As you type or paste the data, it's easy to forget which months have 31 days or on which day of the week the first of a month falls. Excel makes entering such series simple: With AutoFill, you can type a label or value in one cell and assign it to many other cells; type labels or values in two or more cells and have Excel extend the series based on the relationship of the two (or more) cell entries; or even extend dates by a day, a month, or a year.

Fill Data with AutoFill

1 Type the label or value you want to appear in multiple cells.

2 Drag the Fill handle down or across the cells you want to fill.

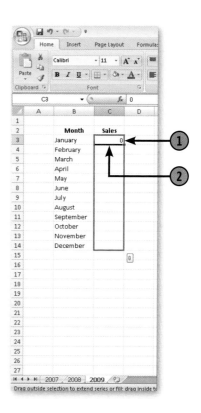

Use AutoFill to Enter a Series of Values

① Type the first label or value for your list.

② Type the second label or value for your list.

③ Select the two cells.

④ Drag the Fill handle to the cell containing the last label or value in the series.

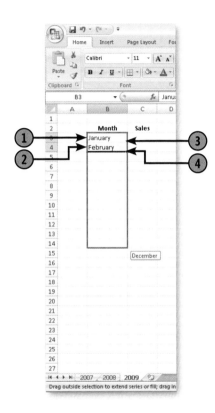

Try This!

Type 1/1/2007 in cell A1 and drag the Fill handle across the cells you want to fill. Excel will fill your cells by increasing the day for every entry. Now click the AutoFill Options button that appears and click Fill Years.

Tip

If you hold down the Ctrl key as you drag the Fill handle, Excel changes how it fills in your series. For example, if dragging the Fill handle would normally copy a single value into the cells you drag over, dragging while holding down the Ctrl key would cause the value to increment (for example, dragging the Fill handle of a cell that contains the value "1" would increment the value to 2, then 3, and so on).

Entering Data with Other Shortcuts

Excel gives you lots of ways to enter data quickly. The less time you spend typing data, the more time you have to analyze and make decisions based on what the data tells you. One way Excel offers to help you enter data is that it recognizes whether the first few characters of the text you're typing matches text from another cell in the same column; if the text matches, Excel offers to complete the rest of that text. If it's the text you want, you can accept it and move on. If not, just keep typing. Do be aware that AutoComplete and Pick from a

Drop-Down List won't work if there's a blank cell in the column above the active cell.

A similar way Excel simplifies data entry is by letting you pick the value for the active cell from a list of existing values in a column. That's not that important for a small worksheet, but when you're working with page after page of data, seeing a sorted list of possible values is a real help.

Enter Data with AutoComplete

1 Type the beginning of an entry.

2 Press Tab to accept the AutoComplete value.

Pick Data from a List

1 Right-click a cell in a column with existing values and click Pick from Drop-Down List from the shortcut menu.

2 Click the item in the list you want to enter.

Caution

AutoComplete will work only if the text or data you are entering is similar to text already in the same column.

Tip

You can also display the Pick from Drop-Down List items by selecting the cell into which you want to enter the value and pressing the Alt+Down Arrow.

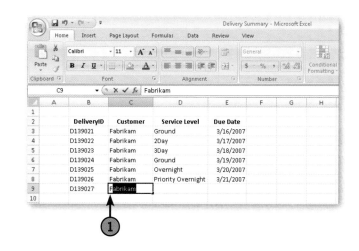

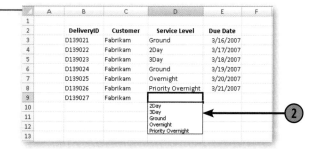

Creating a Data Table

One popular way to maintain data in Excel is by creating a table. A table describes one type of object, such as orders, sales, or contact information. Structurally, a table consists of a header row, which contains labels describing the data in each column, and data rows, which contain data about a particular instance of the table's subject. For example, if you use a table to store your customer's contact information, you could have a separate column for the customer's first name, last name, street address, city, state, postal code, and telephone number. Each row in a table would contain a particular customer's information.

Before Excel 2003, the program didn't have a formal way of dealing with data tables. In Excel 2003 the programming team introduced lists, which were the precursor to tables, but lists didn't have the full range of features realized with Excel 2007 data tables.

Create a Data Table

1. Type your table headers in a single row.

2. Type your first data row directly below the header row.

3. Click any cell in the range from which you want to create a table.

4. On the Home tab, click Format As Table.

5. Click the desired table style.

6. Verify that Excel identified the data range correctly.

7. If your table has headers, select the My Table Has Headers check box.

8. Click OK.

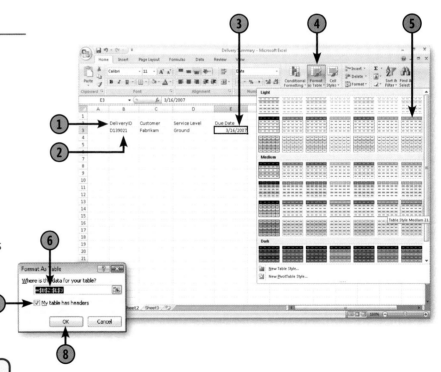

Tip

You can display the Create Table dialog box by clicking any cell in an existing cell range and pressing Ctrl+L.

Add Data to a Data Table

Follow either of these steps:

- Click the cell at the bottom right corner of the data table and press Tab to create a new table row.

- Type data into the cell below the bottom left corner of the data table and press Tab. Excel will make the new row part of the data table.

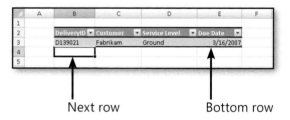

Next row   Bottom row

Rename a Data Table

1. Click any cell in the table.

2. On the ribbon, under Table Tools, click the Design tab.

3. In the Properties group, type a new name for your table and press Enter.

Resize a Table

■ Drag the resize handle at the bottom right corner of the table to add or remove table rows or columns.

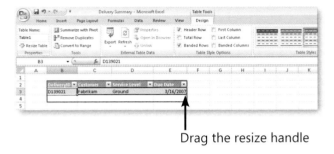

Drag the resize handle

Select a Table Column

■ Click the header of the column you want to select.

Table column header

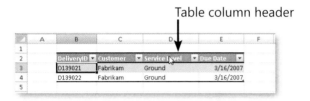

Caution

Be sure not to click the filter arrow at the right edge of a table's column header; doing so displays the column's filter options which, although useful, don't enable you to select the entire column.

Editing Cell Contents

You're not stuck with the first data you enter into a cell. In fact, you can change the value completely, delete it, or update it to reflect a supplier's new business name or a customer's new address. You also are not stuck with only one way to edit the data; you can edit the data either in the Formula Bar or directly in the cell.

Edit Cell Contents in the Formula Bar

① Click the cell you want to edit.

② Select the text you want to edit in the Formula Bar.

③ Type the new text and press Enter.

Edit Cell Contents Directly in the Cell

① Double-click the cell you want to edit.

② Select the text you want to edit.

③ Type the new text and press Enter.

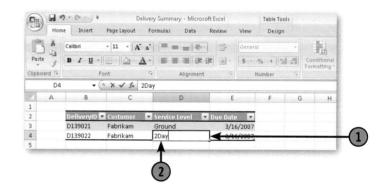

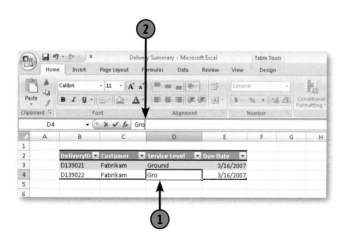

Tip

If you're editing a cell and decide you don't want to keep your edits, press the Esc key to return the cell to its previous state.

Tip

In previous versions of Excel, you needed to select a check box to enable editing directly in a cell. You don't have to check a box in Excel 2007—you can just double-click and edit to your heart's content.

Inserting a Symbol in a Cell

Not every bit of information can be communicated effectively with text. If your worksheet is meant for public consumption and you mention another company's products, you might want to include a trademark (™) or another symbol to rec-ognize that company's intellectual property. Excel—and the other Office programs—has lots of symbols you can use. If you use a symbol in the course of your everyday business, you can probably find it in Excel.

Add a Symbol to a Cell

1. Click the Insert tab.

2. Click Symbol.

3. Click the Font down arrow.

4. Select the font from which you want to pick the symbol.

5. Click the symbol you want to insert.

6. Click the Insert button.

7. Click the Close button.

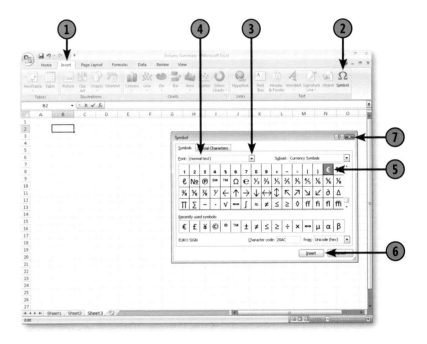

Tip

If you want to insert more than one symbol consecutively (in the same cell), click the first symbol, click the Insert button, click the next symbol, click the Insert button again, and so on. When you're done inserting symbols, click the Close button.

Creating Hyperlinks

One of the hallmarks of the World Wide Web is that documents published on the Web can have references, or hyperlinks, to points in the same document or to other Web documents. One great way to take advantage of this feature would be to create a workbook in which you track sales by product and have a cell at the end of each product's row with

a hyperlink to in-depth product information. That information could be on another worksheet in the same workbook, in another file on your computer, in a file on another computer, or on a Web page. Another type of hyperlink is the mailto hyperlink, which, when clicked, lets you send an e-mail message to the address referred to in the link.

Add a Hyperlink to a Place in the Same File

1. Click the cell where you want to place a hyperlink.

2. Click the Insert tab.

3. Click Hyperlink.

4. Click Place In This Document.

5. Click the sheet to which you want to link.

6. Type the cell reference of the cell to which you want to link.

7. Type a short phrase to describe the hyperlink's target.

8. Click OK.

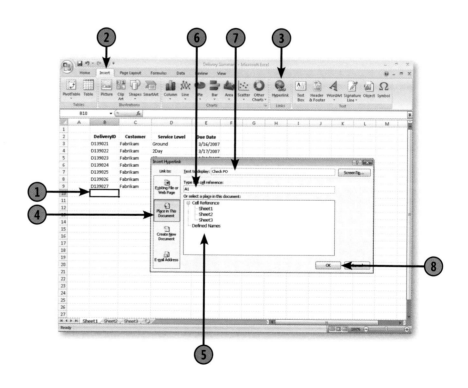

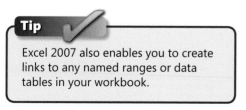

Tip

Excel 2007 also enables you to create links to any named ranges or data tables in your workbook.

Add a Hyperlink to Another File

① Click the cell in which you want to place a hyperlink.

② Click the Insert tab.

③ Click Hyperlink.

④ Click Existing File Or Web Page.

⑤ Click Current Folder.

⑥ Click the file to which you want to link.

⑦ Type a short phrase to describe the hyperlink's target.

⑧ Click OK.

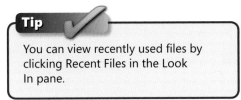

Tip

You can view recently used files by clicking Recent Files in the Look In pane.

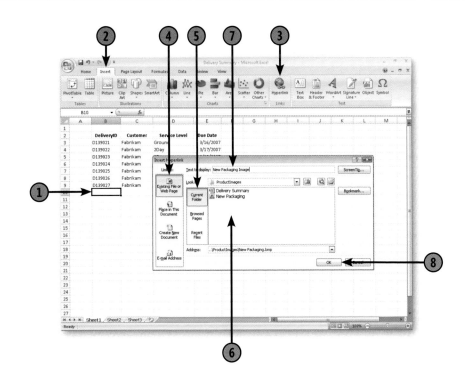

Add a Hyperlink to a Web Page

① Click the cell in which you want to place a hyperlink.

② Click the Insert tab.

③ Click Hyperlink.

④ Click Existing File Or Web Page.

⑤ Click Browsed Pages.

⑥ Click the Web page to which you want to link.

⑦ Type a short phrase to describe the hyperlink's target.

⑧ Click OK.

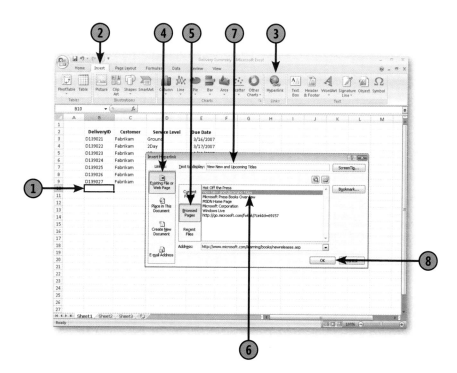

Caution

When you click Browsed Pages, the Insert Hyperlink dialog box displays all of the Web pages you visited recently.

Add a Mailto Hyperlink

1. Click the cell in which you want to place a hyperlink.

2. Click the Insert tab.

3. Click Hyperlink.

4. Click E-Mail Address.

5. Type the e-mail address to which you want to link.

6. Type text describing the hyperlink.

7. Type a default subject for the e-mail message.

8. Click OK.

Tip

You can just type the target e-mail address in the E-Mail Address field. Excel adds the mailto: prefix for you.

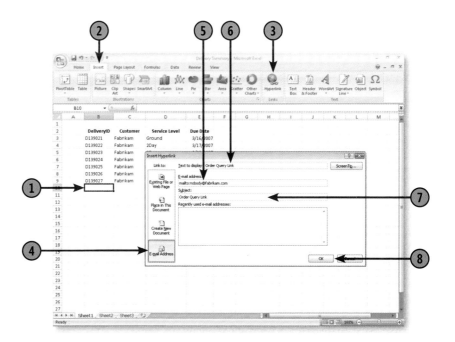

Cutting, Copying, and Pasting Cell Values

After you've entered values into one or more cells, you can copy the values and paste them into another cell, remove the values from the cells and paste them elsewhere, or just cut the values and leave them on the clipboard. Excel 2007 lets you control how the pasted values appear in your worksheet.

When you do paste data you've cut or copied from a cell, Excel displays an option button asking how you want to format the data you're pasting. You can choose to have the data retain its original formatting, adopt the formatting of the cell in which you're pasting the data, or paste the data without formatting.

Cut a Cell Value

1. Select the cells you want to cut.
2. Click the Home tab.
3. In the Clipboard group, click the Cut button.

Copy a Cell Value

1. Select the cells you want to copy.
2. Click the Home tab.
3. In the Clipboard group, click the Copy button.

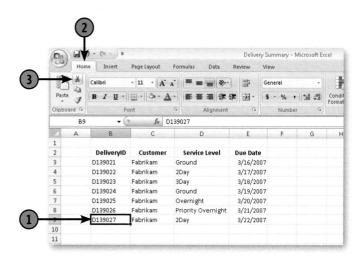

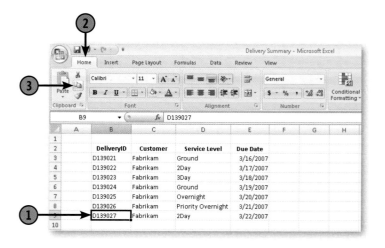

Pasting Values with More Control

When you cut or copy cells, you write a copy of the cells' contents and formatting to the clipboard. When you paste the cells back into a worksheet, Excel pastes the values, formulas, and formatting associated with the cells. You're not limited to such simple pasting behavior, however; you can choose to paste just the cell's formula, just a formula's result, paste everything except the cells' borders, or even paste an image of the item that you can click to display the item you copied.

The following table lists the advanced paste options you can use.

Option	Action
Paste	Performs the standard paste operation.
Formulas	Pastes the formulas from the cells you copied.
Paste Values	If the copied cell contains a formula, pastes the result of the formula into the target cell.
No Borders	Pastes the contents of the copied cells without including any borders drawn around the cells.
Transpose	Exchanges the rows and columns of the copied data.
Paste Link	Creates a link to the copied item; does not create a new copy of the item.
Paste Special	Displays the Paste Special dialog box.
Paste as Hyperlink	Pastes a text hyperlink to the copied item.
Paste as Picture Link	Pastes an image that, when clicked, activates a hyperlink to the copied item.
Paste as Picture	Pastes an image of the copied item's appearance (for example, pasting a picture of a chart doesn't create a new chart).
Copy as Picture	Copies an image of the selected item's appearance to the clipboard.

Paste Values with More Control

① Click the cell in which you want to paste your values.

② Click the Home tab.

③ In the Clipboard group, click the Paste button's down arrow.

④ Select the action you want to take.

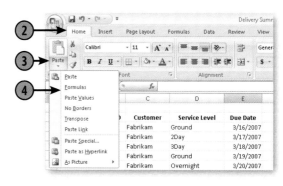

Clearing Cell Contents

If you're lucky, you won't have to replace the data entry and formatting you've entered into a workbook; however, there might be times when you want to clear the data, formatting, or contents of a group of cells. Clearing is like cutting, but clearing differs because it always leaves the formatting in the cell from which you remove the data. When you clear a cell's contents, you have the option of returning the cell to its original state.

Clear a Cell

① Select the cell you want to clear.

② Click the Home tab.

③ In the Editing group, click the Clear button.

④ Select the type of clearing you want.

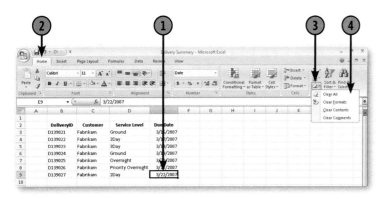

Using the Office Clipboard

When you work in Excel, you can take advantage of the flexibility that comes with its place in the Office suite by using the Office Clipboard. The Office Clipboard keeps track of the last 24 items you've cut or copied from any Office document. You can open the Office Clipboard and then paste any of its contents into your workbook. If an item resides on the Office Clipboard that you know you won't use again, you can always remove it.

Display the Contents of the Office Clipboard

① Click the Home tab.

② Click the Clipboard dialog box launcher.

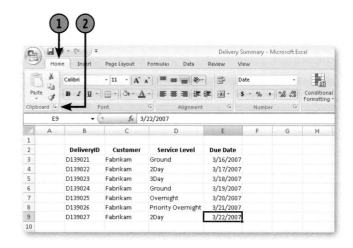

Tip ✔

If all you want to do is clear the cell contents, click the cell you want to clear and then press Delete.

Paste an Item from the Office Clipboard

① Click the cell in which you want to paste a Clipboard item.

② Click the Clipboard item you want to paste.

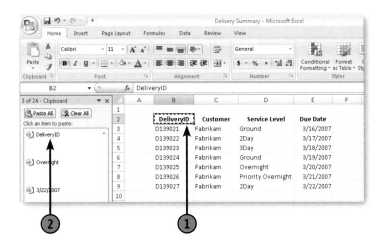

Clear an Item from the Office Clipboard

① Point to the Clipboard item you want to delete.

② Click the down arrow that appears next to the item.

③ Click Delete.

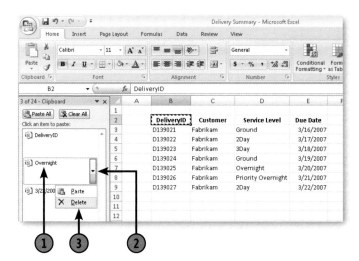

Tip ✔

You can paste every item from the clipboard into your application by clicking Paste All.

Tip ✔

You can remove all entries from the Office Clipboard by clicking Clear All.

Undoing or Redoing an Action

One of the strengths of Excel is that it's easy to change the formatting, layout, and structure of your workbooks. The problem, of course, is that you might not have made the exact change you wanted. If that's the case, and you haven't closed the workbook since you made the change you want to get rid of, you can easily undo your changes by clicking the Undo button in the Quick Access toolbar. Excel keeps a record of your changes, which you can see by clicking the down arrow at the right edge of the Undo button. If you reversed a change by clicking the Undo button, Excel displays the Redo button. Clicking the Redo button, as you might expect, reapplies the last change you undid. If you have made a change but haven't clicked the Undo button, Excel displays the Repeat button, which you can click to apply the last change to a new selection.

Undo or Redo an Action

Follow either of these steps:

- Click the Undo button.
- Click the Redo button.

Undo

Redo

Finding and Replacing Text

After you've entered data into a workbook, you might need to search the document for a particular word or, if one of your suppliers changes the name of a product, replace some or all instances of a word or phrase. You can do just that using Find and Replace in Excel.

Find a Word or Value

1 Click the Home tab.

2 In the Editing group, click Find and Select.

3 Click Find.

4 Type the text you want to find.

5 Click Find Next.

6 Click Close.

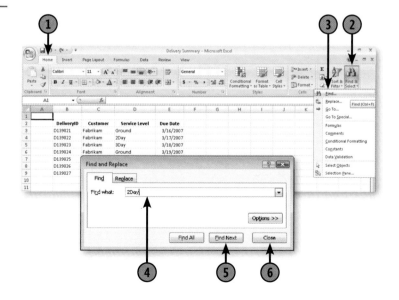

Replace a Word or Value

1. Click the Home tab.

2. In the Editing group, click Find and Select.

3. Click Replace.

4. Type the text you want to replace.

5. Type the text you want to take the place of the existing text.

6. Click Find Next. Follow any of these steps:

   - Click Replace to replace the text.

   - Click Find Next to skip this instance of the text and move to the next time it occurs.

   - Click Replace All to replace every instance of the text.

7. Click Close.

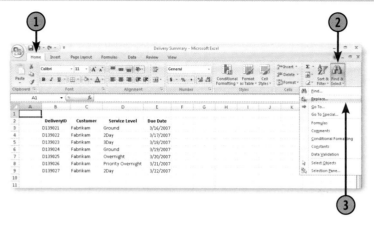

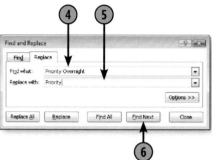

Caution

Clicking Replace All is a quick way to change every occurrence of one value to another value, but it can also have unintended consequences. For example, changing "ear" to "bear" would change "hearing" to "hbearing." It's much safer to use Find Next and verify each change.

Checking the Spelling of Your Worksheet

After you create a workbook and fill it with data, labels, and explanatory text, you should always use the Excel spelling checker to check your text for misspellings. If Excel finds a word it doesn't recognize, the spelling checker will ask you whether it's correct and, if not, might suggest alternatives.

You can have Excel ignore a word once or for the entire document, choose one of the program's suggestions, or even add new words to the dictionary. Products are often given unique names, so adding them to the dictionary Excel uses to check all documents will save you a lot of time.

Check Spelling

1. Click the Review tab.

2. In the Proofing group, click Spelling. If you are asked whether you want to save your work, do so.

3. Follow any of these steps:

   - Click Ignore Once to ignore the current misspelling.

   - Click Ignore All to ignore all instances of the misspelled word.

   - Click Add to Dictionary to add the current word to the dictionary.

   - Click the correct spelling and then click Change to replace the current misspelling with the correct word.

   - Click the correct spelling and then click Change All to replace all instances of the current misspelling with the correct word.

   - Click Cancel to stop checking spelling.

4. Click OK to clear the dialog box that appears after the spelling check is complete.

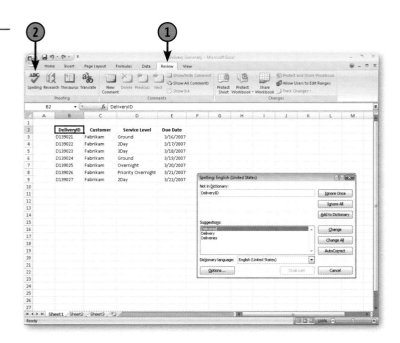

Tip

If you didn't start checking spelling with cell A1 selected, Excel checks spelling to the end of the worksheet and then displays a dialog box asking if you want to continue checking from the beginning of the worksheet. Click Yes to continue.

5

Managing and Viewing Worksheets

After you've built your workbook, you can reorganize it as needed. If you use data in a specific worksheet often, you can move the worksheet to the front of the workbook. Similarly, if you often switch between two worksheets, you can put their sheet tabs next to each other so you don't have to spend as much time moving from one worksheet to the other. Another way you can save time is to enter the same data or apply the same formatting to multiple cells in several worksheets at the same time.

Finally, you can change how Excel displays your data in a workbook. If you have a series of headings in the first row of a worksheet, they don't have to disappear when you scroll down. Instead, you can have Excel *freeze* the rows at the top of the screen and scroll down as far as you want without losing your guides at the top.

Viewing and Selecting Worksheets

Every Excel workbook should hold data on a given subject, such as products you carry, your customers, or sales. By the same token, every page, or worksheet, in a workbook should store part of the workbook's data. One way to divide your data is by time. For example, if you track your sales by the hour, you could easily fit a month's worth of data in a worksheet; at most you would need 31 rows to cover every day and, if your store were open around the clock, 24 columns to take care of the hours. You can view individual worksheets quickly, and it's simple to work with more than one worksheet at a time.

Select Multiple Worksheets

1. Click the sheet tab of the first worksheet you want to select.

2. Hold down the Ctrl key and click the sheet tabs of additional worksheets you want to select.

Tip

To select multiple adjacent worksheets, click the first worksheet, hold down the Shift key, and then click the last sheet tab you want to select.

See Also

For information about adding worksheets to a workbook, see "Inserting or Deleting Worksheets" on page 62.

Tip

You can select all worksheets in a workbook by right-clicking any sheet tab and choosing Select All Sheets from the shortcut menu.

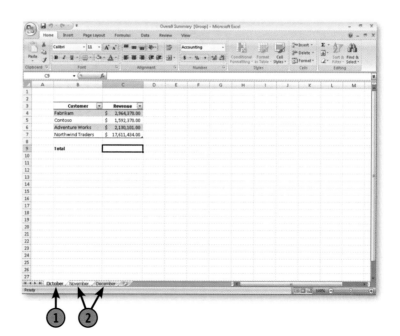

Renaming Worksheets

When you create a workbook, Excel names your worksheets Sheet1, Sheet2, and Sheet3. Those names are fine when you first create a workbook, but after you've added data to several worksheets, naming the sheet tabs will help you and your colleagues find the data for which you're looking. As always, if you think of a better name for your worksheets, or even want to change the name of a worksheet temporarily to make it stand out, you can do so any time you want.

Change the Name of a Worksheet

① Double-click the sheet tab of the worksheet you want to rename.

② Type the new name of the worksheet and press Enter.

Moving Worksheets

Business needs change—the data that was so important yesterday might be of only passing significance today. In fact, if a new customer sends a big order your way, you might spend most of your time adding to and reading from a worksheet you hadn't looked at more than twice in the previous month. If that worksheet is at the back of your workbook, you can move it to the front to make it easier to find in the workbook. Or, if you keep every other worksheet relating to that customer in a separate workbook, you can move the worksheet from its current spot to its rightful place in the other workbook.

Move Worksheets within the Workbook

① Drag the sheet tab of the worksheet you want to move.

Indicator showing where the sheet will be moved

Move Worksheets to Another Workbook

1. Open the workbook that will receive the worksheets.

2. Switch to the workbook that contains the worksheets you want to move, hold down the Ctrl key, and click the sheet tabs of the worksheets you want to move.

3. Right-click the selection.

4. Choose Move Or Copy from the shortcut menu.

5. Click the To Book down arrow.

6. Click the workbook to which you want to move the worksheets.

7. Click OK.

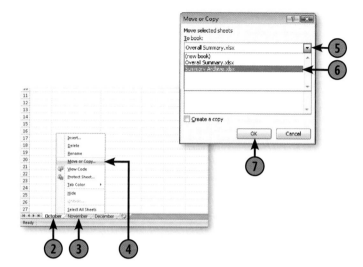

Tip

If you want to position a worksheet last in a workbook, right-click the worksheet you want to move, choose Move Or Copy from the shortcut menu, click Move To End, and click OK.

Tip

If the destination workbook has a different Office theme applied to it, selecting the Match Destination Theme check box causes the copied worksheet to take on the target workbook's formatting.

Copying Worksheets

When you've finished adding data to a worksheet—such as at the end of a calendar month, when you create a new worksheet to store data for the next month—you might want to include the entire worksheet as part of a monthly overview to your general manager. Rather than keep all of the worksheets in their original workbooks and flip from document to document when you create your presentation, you can copy the worksheet from the current workbook (and any other worksheets with data you want to include) to a central document. Going from worksheet to worksheet is much easier than going from workbook to workbook!

Copy Worksheets within the Workbook

Hold the down Ctrl key and drag the worksheet you want to copy to the new location.

Copy Worksheets to Another Workbook

(1) Open the workbook that will receive the new worksheets.

(2) Switch to the workbook that contains the worksheets you want to copy, hold down the Ctrl key, and click the sheet tabs of the worksheets you want to copy.

(3) Right-click the selection.

(4) Choose Move Or Copy from the shortcut menu.

(5) Select the Create A Copy check box.

(6) Click the To Book down arrow.

(7) Click the workbook to which you want the worksheet(s) copied.

(8) Click OK.

Tip

Select the New Book option from the To Book list to copy the worksheet into a new workbook.

Caution

If you don't hold down the Ctrl key while you drag the sheet tab of the worksheet you want to copy, you will just move the worksheet to a new location in the workbook.

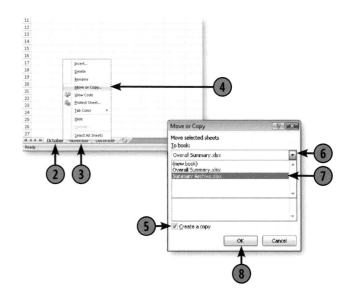

Inserting and Deleting Worksheets

If you haven't changed Excel from the way it was installed, any workbooks you create will contain three worksheets. Three worksheets are plenty of room if you're working at home and are perhaps more than you'll need for small projects, but you'll run out of space quickly if you're tracking products or monthly sales. Adding or deleting a worksheet takes just a moment, but if you want to delete a worksheet, be sure you're getting rid of the right one!

Insert a Blank Worksheet

① Right-click the sheet tab of the worksheet that follows the location where you want to insert a worksheet.

② Choose Insert from the shortcut menu.

③ Double-click Worksheet.

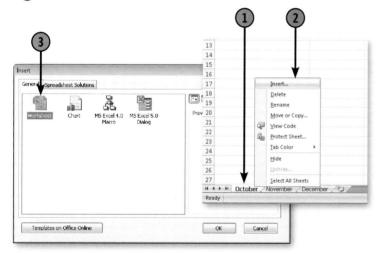

Delete One or More Worksheets

① Hold down the Ctrl key and click the sheet tabs of the worksheets you want to delete.

② Right-click the selection.

③ Choose Delete from the shortcut menu.

④ Click Delete to confirm that you want to delete the worksheet.

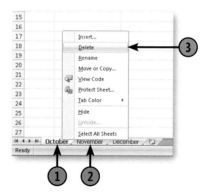

Tip ✔

If you want to insert a worksheet at the end of the workbook, click the Insert Worksheet button at the right edge of the tab bar.

Caution ❗

If you have data in the worksheet that you want to delete, deleting the worksheet will erase all the data in that worksheet. This operation is not reversible.

Hiding or Showing a Worksheet

If you build a workbook that contains a lot of worksheets, you might find it easier to navigate the workbook if you can't see the sheet tabs of the worksheets you're not using. You can hide the sheet tabs of worksheets so they don't appear in the Excel window, reducing the clutter and letting you find the worksheets you are using with no trouble.

Hide or Unhide a Worksheet

(1) Hold down the Ctrl key and click the sheet tabs of the worksheets you want to hide.

(2) Right-click any selected worksheet tab and then choose the Hide command.

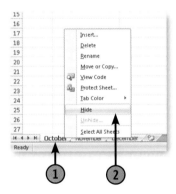

Unhide a Hidden Worksheet

(1) Right-click any worksheet tab.

(2) Click Unhide.

(3) Click the worksheet you want to unhide.

(4) Click OK.

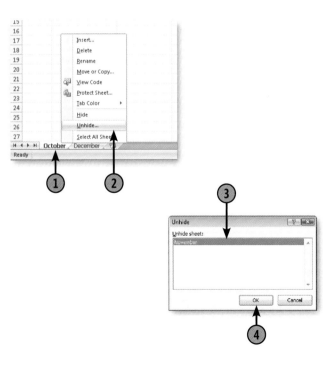

Changing Worksheet Tab Colors

A great way to make any worksheet element stand out is to change it to a color that contrasts with the other colors used in the worksheet. In Excel, you can change the color of sheet tabs. For example, you can change the color of a sheet tab in a workbook in which you track sales for a year, with a worksheet for each month. Rather than move the current worksheet to the front of the list, which would put the worksheets out of order, you can change the color of the sheet tab to make it stand out. When the month ends, you can remove the color from that sheet tab and apply it to the new month's sheet tab.

Color a Sheet Tab

① Hold down the Ctrl key and click the sheet tabs you want to color.

② Right-click the selection and point to Tab Color on the shortcut menu.

③ Select the color you want.

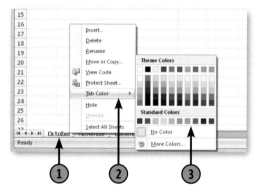

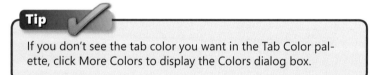

Tip

If you don't see the tab color you want in the Tab Color palette, click More Colors to display the Colors dialog box.

Inserting, Moving, and Deleting Cells

There's very little that's more frustrating than creating a large worksheet and discovering that you forgot to enter data in a few cells. If you're new to Excel, you might be tempted to cut the existing cells and paste them a few cells below their current location to make room for the new data. But that's too much like work; there's an easier way to insert a few cells to give you the room you need. Similarly, it's not that difficult to move a group of cells to a new location in your worksheet or to delete a group of cells that contains data you entered by accident. After you insert or delete cells, you can choose how to move existing cells to fill in the space left by the deleted cells or to make room for the new cells.

Inserting Cells in a Worksheet

① Select the cells in the spot where you want to insert new cells.

② Click the Home tab.

③ In the Cells group, click the Insert button's down arrow.

④ Click Insert Cells.

⑤ Select the option button representing how you want to move the existing cells to make room for the inserted cells.

⑥ Click OK.

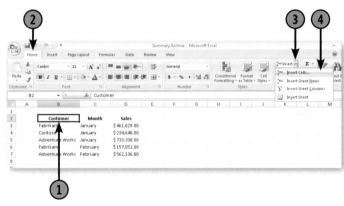

Moving Cells in a Worksheet

① Select the cells you want to move.

② Move the mouse pointer over the outline of the selected cells.

③ Drag the cells to the desired location.

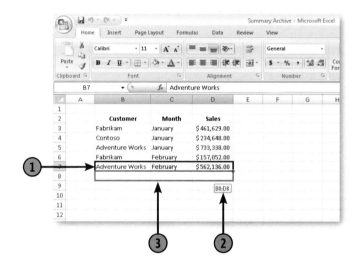

Tip

As you drag the cells in the worksheet, Excel displays an outline where the cells would go when you release the left mouse button.

Deleting Cells in a Worksheet

1 Select the cells you want to delete.

2 Click the Home tab.

3 In the Cells group, click the Delete button's down arrow.

4 Click Delete Cells.

5 Select the option button representing how you want the remaining cells to fill in the deleted space.

6 Click OK.

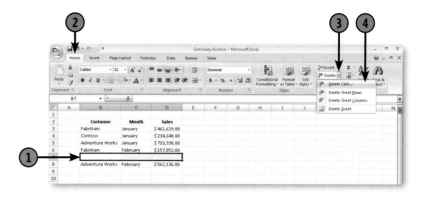

> ### Caution
>
> Because Excel doesn't highlight an entire row or column when you click a single cell, you can be a bit inaccurate if you attempt to delete a row or column by clicking a cell and then clicking the Entire Row or Entire Column option button in the Delete dialog box. It's better to follow the procedure listed in the following section, where you click the row or column header, so you can see the entire row or column to be deleted.

Inserting, Moving, and Deleting Columns and Rows

After you've created a worksheet and begun filling in your data, you might decide to insert a row or column to add data you didn't think to include when you started. For example, a customer might want to add a product to an order. To accommodate this new data, you can insert a blank row below the last row in their existing order and add the new item there. You can do the same with columns; you can even use the Insert Options button to format the new rows or columns.

On the other hand, there might be times when you no longer need to use a particular row or column. Whether you placed an extra column to add some white space between the main body of data and a summary calculation or a row holds the contact information of a customer who has asked to be removed from your list, you can delete either the row or column quickly and easily. Or, if you'd like to change a column or row's position, you can move a group of columns or rows to another location in the worksheet.

Insert a Row in a Worksheet

1. Right-click the row header below where you want the new row to appear.

2. Choose Insert from the shortcut menu.

Insert a Column in a Worksheet

1. Right-click the column header to the right of where you want the new column to appear.

2. Choose Insert from the shortcut menu.

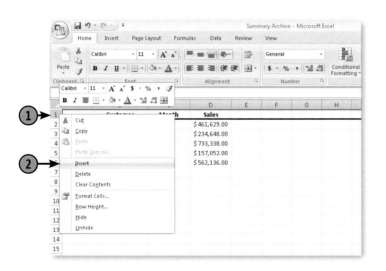

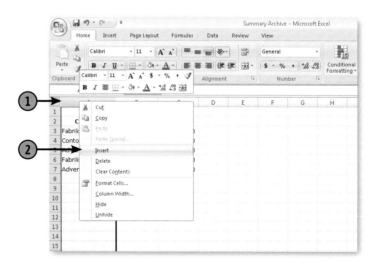

Set Insert Options

1. After inserting rows or columns, click the Insert Options button.

2. Select the type of formatting you want the new cells to have.

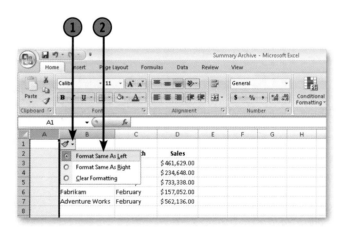

Delete a Row or Column

1. Select the row or column you want to delete.

2. Right-click the selection and choose Delete from the shortcut menu.

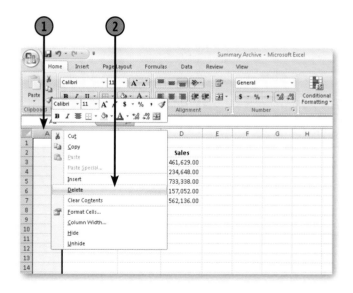

Move One or More Rows

① Select the rows you want to move.

② Click the Home tab.

③ Click the Cut button.

④ Click the first cell in the row where you want the rows to be moved.

⑤ Click the Paste button.

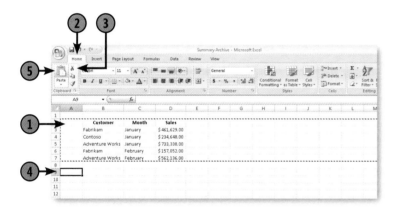

Move One or More Columns

① Select the columns you want to move.

② Click the Home tab.

③ Click the Cut button.

④ Click the first cell in the column where you want to move the columns.

⑤ Click the Paste button.

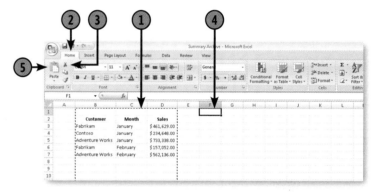

Hiding and Unhiding Columns and Rows

If you're working with a worksheet that contains lots of data, you might need to refer to the contents of rows or columns that aren't close enough on the worksheet to appear on the same screen. Rather than scrolling back and forth to access the data you need, you can hide any intervening rows or columns so that everything you need to see is displayed on the screen at the same time. The rows you hide are only gone temporarily. The data hasn't been deleted; it's just been moved out of your way while you don't need it.

Hide Rows or Columns

1. Select the rows or columns you want to hide.

2. Right-click a row or column header in the selection and choose Hide from the shortcut menu.

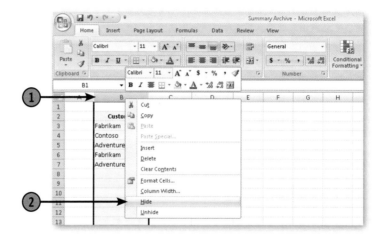

Unhide Rows or Columns

(1) Click the row or column header of the row above or the column to the left of the rows or columns you want to unhide.

(2) Hold down the Shift key and click the row or column header of the row or column below or to the right of the rows or columns you want to unhide.

(3) Right-click the selection and choose Unhide from the shortcut menu.

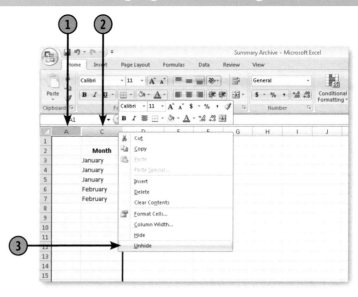

Tip

There are two ways you can tell that hidden rows or columns are in a worksheet. First, whenever rows or columns are hidden, there will be row numbers or column letters missing. For example, if rows 2, 3, and 4 are hidden, the first two visible rows of the worksheet will be labeled row 1 and row 5.

The other way you can tell that a worksheet contains hidden rows or columns is that a thick line will appear on the border of the row header or column header where the rows or columns would otherwise appear.

Entering Data and Formatting Many Worksheets at the Same Time

After you've worked with Excel for a while, you'll probably develop standard worksheets you use over and over. When working with worksheets that follow a common layout, you might want to enter a set of data across multiple worksheets. For example, you might have a set of column headers you want to appear on several worksheets, and you would like to avoid creating them from scratch for each individual worksheet. In Excel 2007, you can save lots of time by entering data and formatting in equivalent blocks of cells on multiple worksheets. If you have existing data you want to paste into several worksheets at the same time, you can do that as well.

Enter and Format Data on Several Worksheets at One Time

① Hold down the Ctrl key and click the sheet tabs of the worksheets you want to edit.

② Select the cell or cells into which you want to enter the data.

③ Type the data you want to appear in the same cell or cells on the worksheets you selected.

④ Right-click the selected cells.

⑤ Using the Mini toolbar, specify the formatting options you want.

⑥ Press Enter.

⑦ Click the sheet tab of any unselected worksheet.

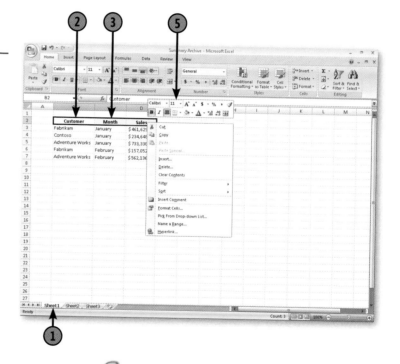

Tip

If you would like to format your cells using controls that aren't available in the Mini toolbar, right-click the cell(s) and choose Format Cells to display the Format Cells dialog box.

Tip

If you selected all of your workbook's worksheets, you can ungroup them by right-clicking any selected worksheet's sheet tab and then clicking Ungroup Sheets.

Copy Cells from One Worksheet to a Group of Worksheets

1 Click the Home tab.

2 Select the cells you want to copy.

3 Click the Copy button.

4 Hold down the Ctrl key and click the sheet tabs of the worksheets you want to receive the copied data.

5 Click the cell you want to receive the data.

6 Click the Paste button.

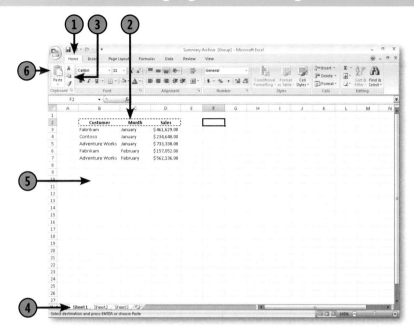

Changing How You Look at Excel Workbooks

When you're examining your Excel data to make a business decision, you'll probably need to look at data from more than one worksheet, or even more than one workbook. Hourly sales totals can help determine when you need more staff on the floor, but if you keep track of the number of customers in the store as well, you might find that your great sales on Monday mornings come from landscape architects loading up for the week. In that case, you would be better off having your ware-house staff and not your counter clerks show up to handle the load.

You can open more than one workbook at a time and arrange them on the screen so you can read data from both sources at the same time. You can do something similar if you have relevant data in two parts of the same worksheet. If you can't see everything you need to see, you can *split* the worksheet into two or four units, all with independent scroll bars.

View Different Parts of One Worksheet at the Same Time

① Click the cell where you want to split the worksheet.

② Click the View tab.

③ In the Window group, click Split.

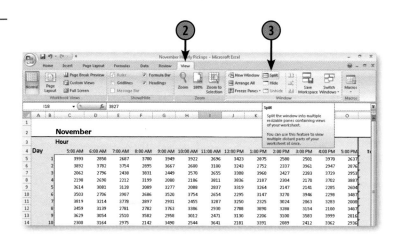

Tip

To remove a worksheet split, click the View tab and then, in the Window group, click Split.

Tip

To split a worksheet into two regions instead of four, click the first cell in the row or column where you want to create the split.

View Multiple Workbooks at the Same Time

1 Open all the workbooks you want to view.

2 Click the View tab.

3 Click Arrange All.

4 Select the option representing the target arrangement.

5 Click OK.

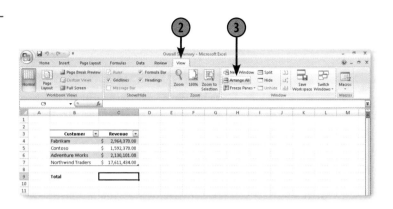

Caution

All of the workbooks will now be arranged like this unless you select the Windows Of Active Workbook check box, which will apply the arrangement only to the active workbook.

View Multiple Parts of a Worksheet by Freezing Panes

1. Click the cell below and to the right of where you want to freeze the worksheet.

2. Click the View tab.

3. In the Window group, click Freeze Panes.

4. Click one of the following items:

   - Freeze Panes, which keeps the cells above or to the left of the current selection visible at all times

   - Freeze Top Row, which keeps the top row visible at all times

   - Freeze First Column, which keeps the left-most column visible at all times

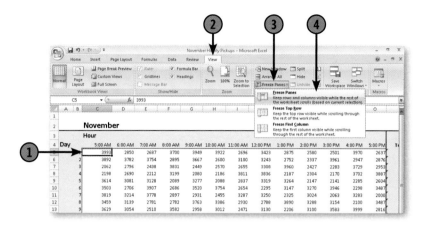

Naming and Using Worksheet Views

After you've set up your Excel worksheets so that you can read them effectively, you don't need to re-create the arrangement every time you run Excel. Instead, you can record the arrangement, which includes splits, frozen rows and columns, and hidden cells, in a view. Views are especially handy for worksheets that will be used by different people, all of whom need different information. Different views can be created for each person, so if the data one person would view spans many columns, you can set the print settings to Landscape mode for that view.

Name the Current View of the Worksheet

1. Arrange your Excel window as you would like it to appear.

2. Click the View tab.

3. Click Custom Views.

4. Click Add.

5. Type the name of the view.

6. Select what you want included in the view.

7. Click OK.

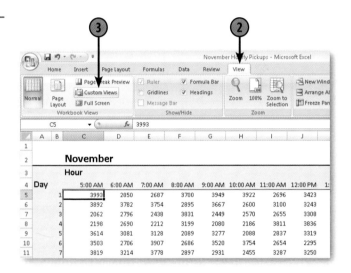

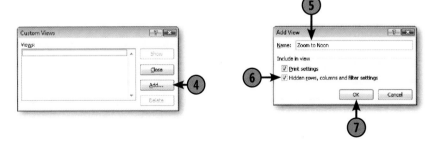

Switch to Another View
of the Worksheet

1 Click the View tab.

2 Click Custom Views.

3 Click the view you want.

4 Click Show.

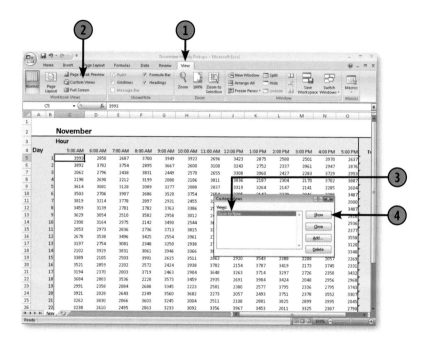

Tip

To delete a custom view, on the View tab, in the Workbook Views group, click Custom Views. Then, in the Custom Views dialog box, click the View you want to delete and then click Delete. Click Yes to verify that you want to delete the custom view and then click Close.

Caution

You can't create a custom view in a workbook that contains an Excel 2007 data table.

6

Using Formulas and Functions

Microsoft Excel workbooks allow you to do much more than simply store and organize your data. One important task you can perform in Excel is to summarize the values in related cells. Whether those cells represent the sales for a day at your store, the returns from your personal investments, or your times in bicycle races, you can find the total or average of the values, identify the minimum or maximum value in a group, or perform dozens of other calculations on your data. Many times you can't access the information you want without referencing more than one cell, and it's also often true you'll use the data in the same group of cells in more than one calculation. Excel makes it easy to reference a number of cells at once, letting you build your calculations quickly.

Understanding Formulas and Cell References in Excel

After you've added your data to a worksheet, you can summarize the data by creating *formulas*. A formula is an expression that performs calculations on your data. For example, in a worksheet that lists hourly sales for a day in a single row of cells, you can build a formula in the last cell in that row to find the total of all sales for the day. You can also build the formula to calculate the average or find the lowest or highest hourly value.

When you build a formula, you need to identify the worksheet cells that will provide the values for the formula and the operations you want performed on those values. To identify a cell, you give its *cell reference.* The first cell in the first column is cell A1, meaning column A, row 1. If you examine a formula, you will sometimes see a cell reference written as $A$1, rather than just A1. The difference is that cell references written with the dollar signs are *absolute references*, meaning the reference won't change when the formula is copied to another cell, and cell references written without the dollar signs are *relative references*, which will change when the formula with the references is copied to another cell.

The benefit of relative references is that you can write a formula once, copy it to as many other cells as you like, and have Excel update the formulas to reflect their new cells. As an example, consider the worksheet in the figure, which tracks the number of hourly package pickups for a month.

The cells in column P contain formulas that calculate the sum of the hourly pickup values in column C through column O. The formula in cell P5, =SUM(C5:O5), finds the sum of cells in row 5, corresponding to October 1. When you copy the formula from cell P5 to cell P6, the formula changes to =SUM(C6:O6). Excel notices that you copied the formula to a new row and assumes that you want the formula to work on that data. Had you written the formula as =SUM($C$5:$O$5), however, Excel would notice that the formula used absolute references and would copy the formula as =SUM($C$5:$O$5).

If you want to reference a value from a cell in another workbook, you can do it. Excel uses *3D references*, which means that any cell in any workbook can be described by three pieces of information:

- The name of the workbook
- The name of the worksheet
- The cell reference

Here's the reference for cell Q38 on the January worksheet in the Y2007ByMonth workbook:

```
[Y2007ByMonth.
xlsx]January!$Q$38
```

The good news is that you don't need to remember how to create these references yourself. If you want to use a cell from another workbook in a formula, all you need to do is click the cell where you'll use the value, start the formula, and click the cell in the other workbook. Excel will fill in the reference for you.

Creating Simple Cell Formulas

Building calculations in Excel is pretty straightforward. If you want to find the sum of the values in two cells, you just type an equal sign (=), the reference of the first cell, a plus sign (+),

and the reference of the second cell. The formula you enter will appear on the formula bar, where you can examine and edit it.

Build a Formula

(1) Click the cell into which you want to enter a formula.

(2) Type =.

(3) Type the expression representing the calculation you want to perform.

(4) Press Enter.

Edit a Formula

(1) Click the cell you want to edit.

(2) Select the part of the formula you want to edit in the formula bar.

(3) Make any changes that you want.

(4) Press Enter.

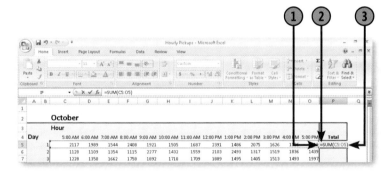

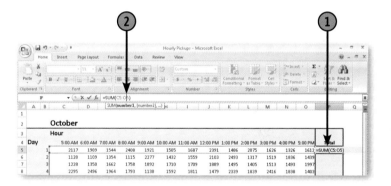

Try This!

Click the Microsoft Office Excel Help button and then, in the Excel Help dialog box, type *common formulas* in the Search text field, press Enter, and then click Examples Of Commonly Used Formulas from the list of available topics. The Microsoft Help file that appears has quite a few examples of formulas you might want to create.

Caution

Be sure that there's no space before the equal sign in your formula. If there is, Excel will interpret the cell's contents as text, not a formula.

Assigning Names to Groups of Cells

When you work with large amounts of data, it's easy to lose track of which cells contain which data. In addition, it can be difficult to locate data in workbooks you didn't create. Although you might always store product prices in one worksheet column, there's no guarantee that your colleagues will follow the same pattern! One way to prevent confusion is to define a *named range* for any cell group that holds specific information. For example, in a worksheet with customer order data, you can define the Totals named range to represent the cells in which the total for each order is stored. After you've defined the named range, you can display its contents, rename it, or delete it.

Create a Named Range

① Select the cells you want to name.

② Click the Name Box on the Formula Bar.

③ Type the name you want for the range.

④ Press Enter.

> **See Also**
>
> For information about selecting cells from several parts of the same worksheet, see "Select a Noncontiguous Group of Cells" on page 34.

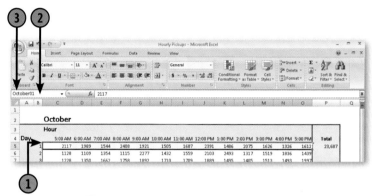

Go to a Named Range

① Click the Name Box down arrow.

② Click the range to which you want to go.

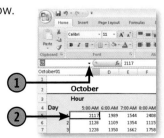

> **Caution**
>
> The name you give your named range shouldn't duplicate a potential cell address. For example, typing *DAY1* in a formula would reference cell DAY1. To avoid this problem, either ensure that your ranges have names that begin with at least four letters (the last column is XFD) or use an underscore to separate the letters from the rest of the name. The name DAY1 isn't valid, but the name DAY_1 is.

Delete a Named Range

1. Click the Formulas tab.

2. Click Name Manager.

3. Click the named range you want to delete.

4. Click Delete.

5. Click OK to clear the confirmation dialog box that appears.

6. Click Close.

Rename a Named Range

1. Click the Formulas tab.

2. Click Name Manager.

3. Click the named range you want to rename.

4. Click Edit.

5. Type a new name for the range.

6. Click OK.

7. Click Close.

Tip

The Name Manager lists the available names in your workbook. That list contains a column named Refers To, which indicates whether any formulas use a range to compute the formula's result.

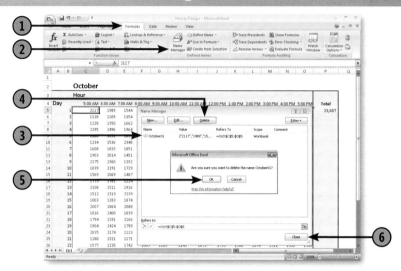

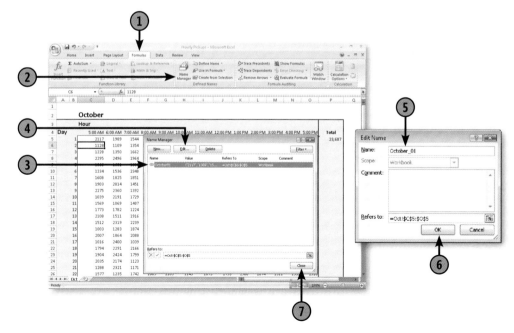

Using Names in Formulas

When you define a named range, you create a shortcut that you can use to refer to a group of cells. A great way to use named ranges is in formulas. Instead of entering the references of every cell you want to use in your calculation, you can type in the name of the range. When you reference named ranges in formulas, your formulas will be shorter and easier to understand. Rather than seeing a series of cell references you need to examine, you and your colleagues can rely on the named ranges to understand the goal of a calculation.

Excel 2007 further streamlines formula creation with Formula AutoComplete. Remember that when you start typing a value into a cell, Excel examines the previous values in that column and offers to let you complete the entry by pressing Tab or Enter. Now, when you start typing a named range's name into a formula, Excel recognizes that you might be entering a named range and displays a list of named ranges (as well as built-in functions) available in the active workbook. All you have to do is click the named range you want, and it's included in the formula immediately.

Create a Formula with a Named Range

① Click the cell into which you want to enter a formula.

② Type = followed by the formula you want. When you want to use a range that has a name, start typing the name instead of the cell address.

③ Click the desired named range from the Formula Auto-Complete list that appears.

④ Press Enter.

Tip

If you change the name of a range of cells, Excel will automatically make the name change in every one of your formulas.

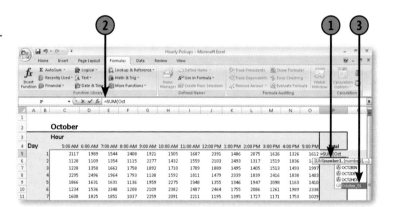

Creating a Formula that References Values in a Table

In previous versions of Excel, it was a challenge to create named ranges that included an entire column in a data list. Suppose that you created a named range that encompassed the existing cells in a data column, such as the cell range A3: A44; if you added data to cell A45, you would need to change

the cells in the named range's definition. Yes, there is a complicated way to create a dynamic named range in Excel 2003 and earlier versions, but you don't have to worry about it in Excel 2007. All you need to do is create a data table (as shown in "Creating a Data Table" on page 41) and select the headers of the columns that contain the data you want to summarize in your formulas.

Create a Formula with a Table Reference

① Click the cell in which you want to create the formula.

② Type =, followed by the function to include in the formula and a left parenthesis; for example, **=SUM(** would be a valid way to start.

③ Move the mouse pointer over the header of the table column you want to use in the formula. When the mouse pointer changes to a black, downward-pointing arrow, click the column header.

④ Type a right parenthesis and press Enter.

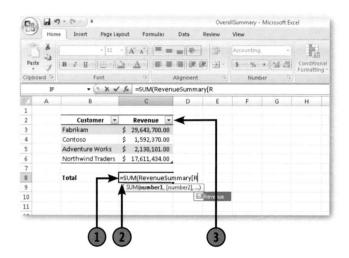

Tip

To include more than one table column in a formula, either hold down the Shift key, select the column header of the first column to use in the formula and click another column to select everything in the span between the two columns, or hold down the Ctrl key and click the other column headers you would like to use. Excel will include the references in the formula.

Creating Formulas that Reference Cells in Other Workbooks

One of the strengths of Excel is that you aren't limited to using cells from the current workbook in your formulas. If you want, you can use data from any other workbook in your calculations. For example, you might have a workbook in which you track monthly advertising sales for your newsletter. If you want to create a new workbook to summarize all income and expenses for your publication, you can do so. By letting you create formulas that reference cells from more than one workbook, Excel makes it easy for you to organize your workbooks so that each workbook holds data about a specific subject. Not only can you find the data easily, you can reference it anywhere else.

After you've created links between workbooks, you can have Excel update your calculation if the data in the linked cell has changed. You can also change the cell to which you've linked or, if the workbook with the cell to which you were linking has been moved or deleted, you can delete the link and have Excel store the last value from the calculation.

Use Cells from Other Workbooks in a Formula

1. Open the workbook with the cell you want to reference in your formula.

2. In the workbook where you want to create the formula, click the View tab.

3. Click Arrange All.

4. Select the Tiled option.

5. Click OK.

(continued on the next page)

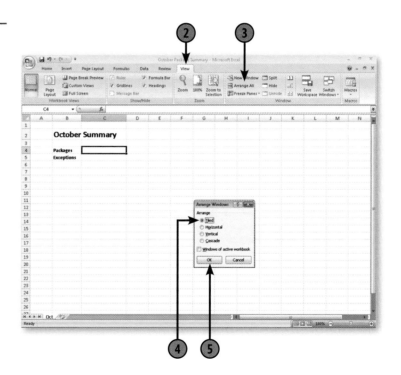

Use Cells from Other Workbooks
in a Formula *(continued)*

6 Click the cell where you want to create the formula.

7 Type = followed by the first part of the formula.

8 Select the cells with the values you want to use in the formula.

9 Press Enter.

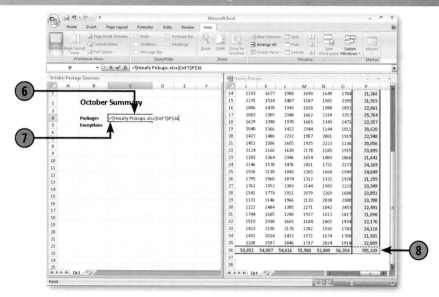

Break Links to Other Workbooks and Convert to Values

1 Click the cell that contains the formula you want to edit.

2 Select the part of the formula representing the link you want to break.

3 Press F9.

4 Press Enter.

Tip

You can use the techniques here to link to a cell on a different worksheet in the same workbook. Just create the formula and, when you want to put in the cell reference, move to the target worksheet and click the appropriate cell.

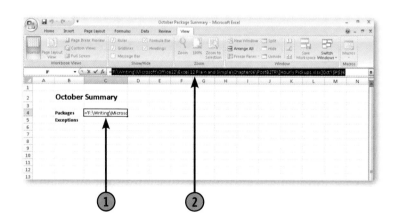

Refresh Links

1. Click the Data tab.
2. In the Connections group, click Edit Links.
3. Click Update Values.
4. Click Close.

Changing Links to Different Workbooks

1. Click the Data tab.
2. In the Connections group, click Edit Links.
3. Click the link you want to change.
4. Click Change Source.
5. Click the workbook with the new cell to which you want to link.
6. Click OK.
7. Click Close.

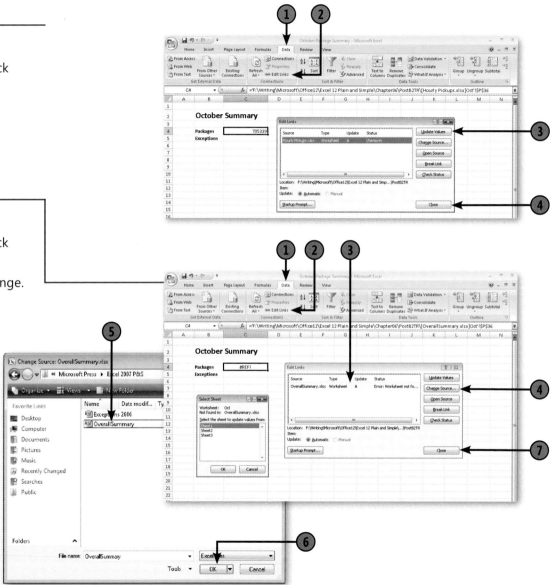

Summing a Group of Cells without Using a Formula

Sometimes, such as when you're entering data into a worksheet or you're curious to find out the sum or average of the values in a few cells, it's too much work to find a blank cell and write a formula to calculate the sum or average for the cells. Rather than make you create a separate formula, Excel counts the number of cells selected, calculates a running total

and average for the currently selected cells, and displays the results on the status bar. Finding the sum, average, and count of the values in the selected cells are the most commonly used operations, so Excel calculates those values by default. You can choose from several other operations, however, or even tell Excel not to calculate a running total for any selected cells.

Summarizing Data in a Group of Cells

(1) Select the cells you want to summarize.

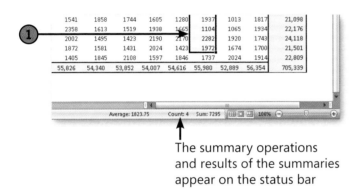

The summary operations and results of the summaries appear on the status bar

Tip

Active summary operations are checked on the shortcut menu. Clicking a checked summary operation turns off that operation.

Find the Total, Average, or Other Values of Cell Data

(1) Right-click the status bar and choose the summary operations you want from the shortcut menu.

Creating a Summary Formula

After you've entered data into a worksheet, you can create formulas to summarize the values and display the result of the calculation. You can summarize the values in a group of cells in many ways: You can find the total or average of the cell values, identify the maximum or minimum value in the group, or simply count the number of cells containing values. You can create these formulas by clicking the cell below or to the right of the cells you want to summarize, displaying either the Home tab or the Formulas tab, and clicking the AutoSum button (the button appears on both tabs). Clicking the AutoSum button itself creates a SUM formula, which finds the arithmetic sum of the values, but you can choose other calculations by clicking the AutoSum button's down arrow. After you've created the formula you want, you can use the result in other calculations.

Create an AutoSum Function

1. Click the cell where you want the summary value to appear.

2. Click the Home tab.

3. Click the AutoSum down arrow.

4. Click the AutoSum function you want to use.

5. If necessary, select the cells with the data you want to summarize.

6. Press Enter.

> **See Also**
>
> For information about finding a running total for a group of cells without creating a formula, see "Summing a Group of Cells without Using a Formula" on page 89.

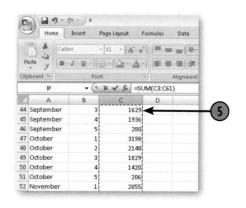

Summing with Subtotals and Grand Totals

You frequently will need to organize the data in an Excel worksheet by one or more criteria. For example, you might have a worksheet in which you list yearly sales for each product you offer, with the products broken down by category. If your data is organized this way, you can have Excel calculate a subtotal for each category of products. When you create a subtotal, you identify the cells with the values to be calculated and the cells that identify the change from one category to the next; Excel will update the subtotal and grand total for you if the value of any cell changes.

Create a Subtotal

① Click any cell in the range you want to subtotal.

② Click the Data tab.

③ In the Outline group, click Subtotal.

④ Click the At Each Change In down arrow.

⑤ Click the value on which you want to base the subtotals.

⑥ Click the Use Function down arrow.

⑦ Click the subtotal function you want to use.

⑧ Select which columns should have subtotals calculated.

⑨ Click OK.

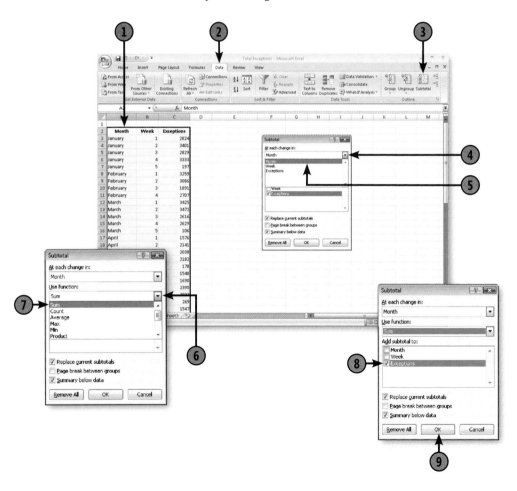

Remove a Subtotal

1 Click any cell in the subtotaled range.

2 Click the Data tab.

3 Click Subtotal.

4 Click Remove All.

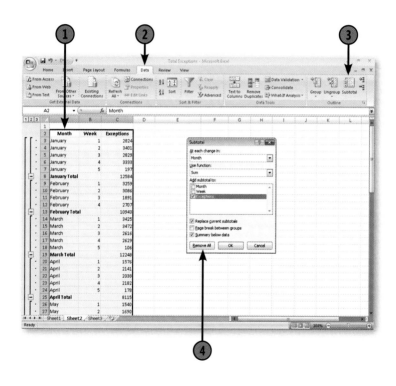

Exploring the Excel Function Library

You can create dozens of different functions in Excel. You can use Excel functions to determine mortgage payments, perform scientific calculations, or find the square root of a number. The best way to become familiar with the formulas available in Excel is to display the Insert Function dialog box and move through the listed functions, clicking the ones that look interesting. When you click a function, its description appears at the bottom of the dialog box.

Another way to get information about a function is to view the ScreenTip that appears next to the function. If you double-click a cell with a function, a ScreenTip with the function's structure and expected values appears below it. Clicking an element of the structure points to the cell or cells providing that value.

List Functions Available from the Excel Library

① Click the Insert Function button.

② Display the drop-down list and click the function category you want to view.

③ Click the function you want to examine.

④ Click OK.

⑤ Click Cancel to close the Function Arguments dialog box.

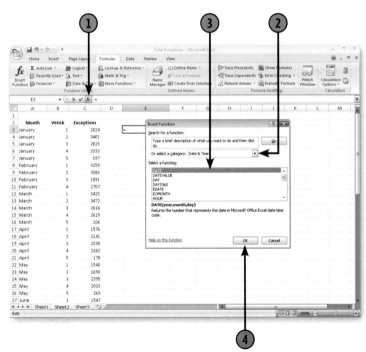

Use Function ScreenTips

① Double-click a cell that contains a formula.

② Click the function name to open the Help file entry for the function.

③ After the Excel Help window closes, click the cell that contains the formula.

④ Click an argument to select the cells to which it refers.

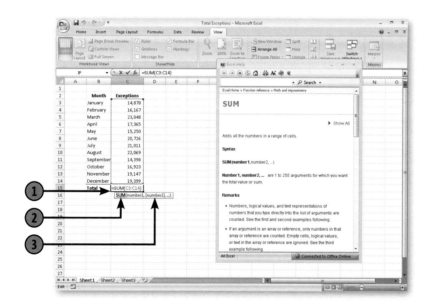

Using the IF Function

In addition to calculating values based on the contents of other cells, you can have Excel take different actions based on the contents of those other cells by using the IF function. For example, if you create a workbook to track the times of riders in a bicycle-racing club, you can create a formula to compare each rider's time to their previous times. When someone's most recent time is the lowest time in the group, you can have Excel display *Personal Best* in the cell with the formula, alerting you to congratulate the rider in your next club newsletter.

Create an IF Function

① Click the cell in which you want to enter an IF function.

② Click the Formulas tab.

③ Click Logical.

④ Click IF.

⑤ Type a conditional statement that evaluates to true or false.

⑥ Type the text you want to appear if the condition is true.

⑦ Type the text you want to appear if the condition is false.

⑧ Click OK.

Caution

The text message must be enclosed in quotes.

Tip

You can also create an expression in the Value_if_true and Value_if_false boxes. Excel will display the result of the expression in the appropriate box.

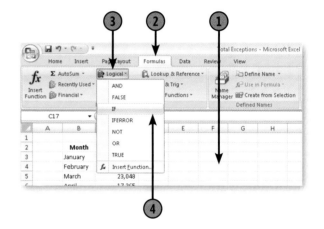

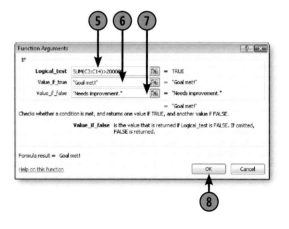

Checking Formula References

When you create a formula that draws values from several different places in your workbook, or from other workbooks, it can be difficult to see what's going wrong if your formula isn't producing the expected results. Excel helps you locate a cell's *precedents* (the cells the formula uses in its calculation)

and *dependents* (the cells that depend on the current cell to calculate their own values). To help you find what you need to check your formulas, Excel groups all of the tools you need on the Formula Auditing group on the Formulas tab.

Find Cell Precedents and Dependents

① Click the cell you want to track.

② Click the Formulas tab.

③ Using the controls in the Formula Auditing group, follow either of these steps:

- ■ Click the Trace Precedents button.

- ■ Click the Trace Dependents button.

Remove Tracer Arrows

① Click the Formulas tab.

② Click the Remove Arrows down arrow and follow any of these steps:

- ■ Click Remove Arrows to remove all arrows.

- ■ Click Remove Precedent Arrows to remove the precedent arrows.

- ■ Click Remove Dependent Arrows to remove the dependent arrows.

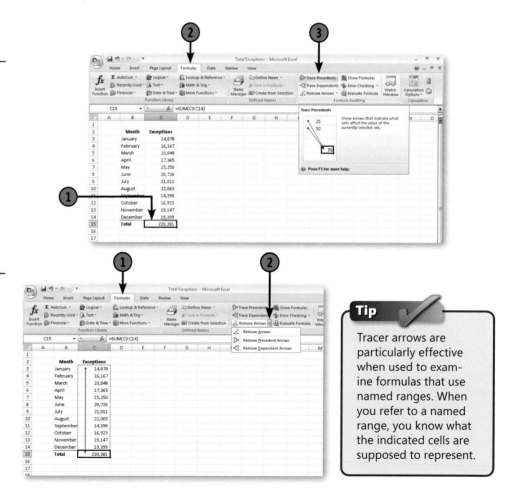

Tip

Tracer arrows are particularly effective when used to examine formulas that use named ranges. When you refer to a named range, you know what the indicated cells are supposed to represent.

Debugging Your Formulas

When you share a workbook with your colleagues, some of the values in that workbook might change rapidly as new data is entered. For example, workbook data probably will change quickly if you are evaluating stock prices. Stock market values change frequently, so your data will as well. You can monitor the value in a cell even while you're using another workbook by setting a *watch*. When you set a watch, the values of the cells you're monitoring appear in the Watch Window.

Another way you can monitor your data is to check the result of part of a calculation using the Evaluate Formula dialog box. When you click the Evaluate Formula button, Excel displays the formula in the active cell and the subtotal for part of the calculation. You can move through the formula bit by bit, with Excel showing you the result of each piece of the formula.

Monitor a Formula for Changes

1. Click the Formulas tab.

2. Click Watch Window.

3. Click Add Watch.

4. Select the cells you want to watch.

5. Click Add.

6. Click Watch Window.

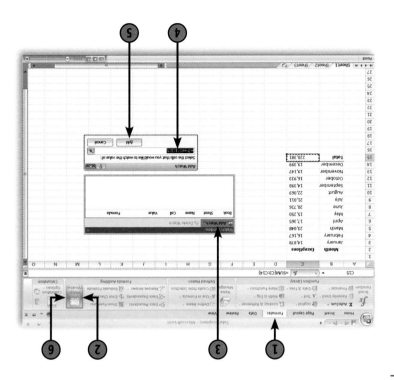

Delete a Watch

1 Click the Formulas tab.

2 Click Watch Window.

3 Click the watch you want to delete.

4 Click Delete Watch.

5 Click the Close button.

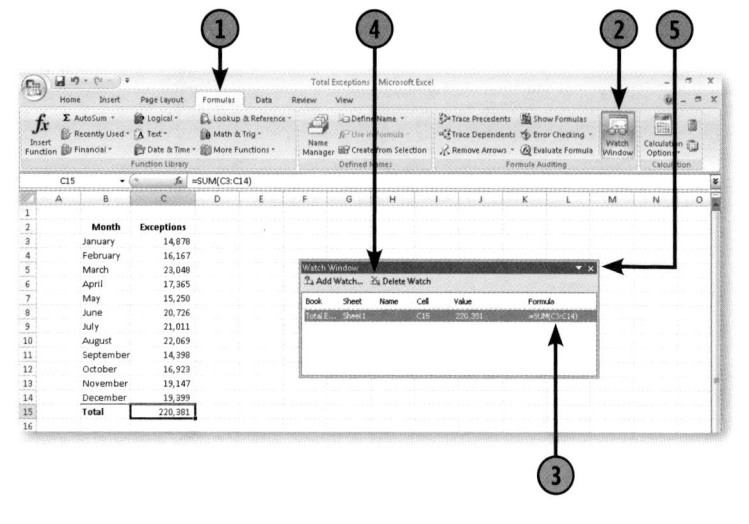

Evaluate Parts of a Formula

1 Click the cell with the formula you want to evaluate.

2 Click the Formulas tab.

3 Click Evaluate Formula.

4 Click Evaluate (one or more times) to move through the formula's elements.

5 Click Close.

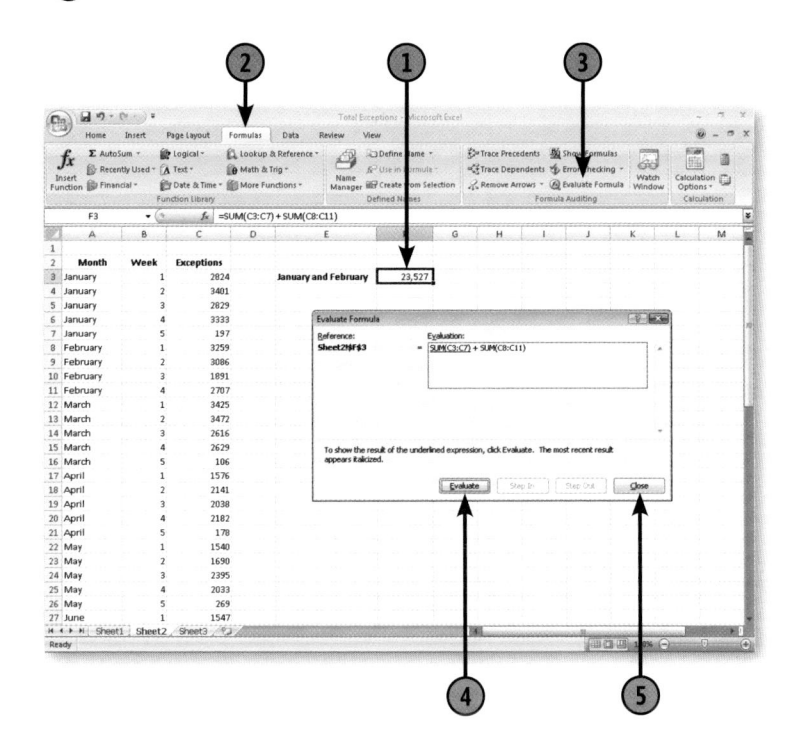

7

Formatting the Worksheet

Microsoft Office Excel 2007 helps you manage large quantities of data with ease. One of the ways you can accomplish this is by changing how the program displays the data in your worksheet. For example, you can easily change the size of characters displayed in a cell, add color to emphasize important cells, or change the orientation of text within a cell. Excel 2007 also enables you to change a cell's formatting based on the contents of the cell by creating conditional formats. While you had the ability to create these conditional formats in previous versions of Excel, Excel 2007 greatly expands the type and number of formats you can create.

Formatting Cell Contents

Some cells have values that need to stand out. Whether the value is a grand total for a year's sales or a label that lets your colleagues know that data entered into the worksheet must be within certain limits, you can change the font used to display the data; make the text larger or smaller; or make the text appear bold, italicized, or underlined. You can apply these settings by using the controls on the Home tab of the ribbon or on the Mini toolbar, but formatting cell contents isn't an all-or-nothing proposition. You can choose to format a word or even a single character in a cell.

Change Font and Font Size

1. Select the cells you want to format.

2. Click the Home tab.

3. Click the Font down arrow.

4. Click the font you want.

5. Click the Font Size down arrow.

6. Click the font size you want.

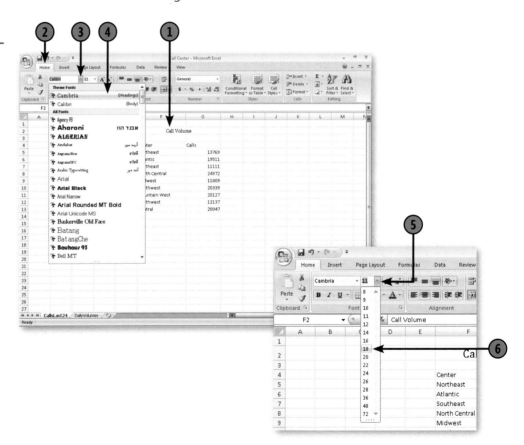

Tip

You can display the Format Cells dialog box, which contains a wider range of cell formatting controls, by selecting a group of cells, right-clicking any selected cell, and choosing Format Cells. You can also display the Format Cells dialog box by clicking the Font group's dialog box launcher.

Change Text Appearance

① Select the cells you want to format.

② Click the Home tab.

③ Use the tools in the Font, Alignment, and Number groups to change your text's appearance.

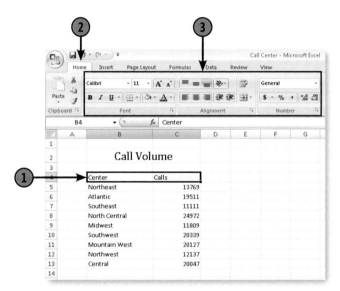

Format Part of a Cell's Contents

① Click the cell with the data you want to format.

② Select the contents of the cell you want formatted on the formula bar.

③ If necessary, click the Home tab.

④ Use the controls in the Font group on the ribbon to apply the changes you want.

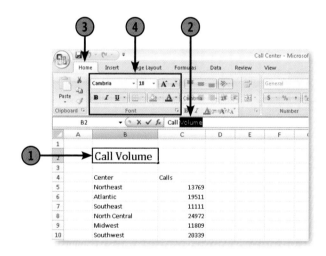

Caution

When you select multiple cells to change their appearance, the range you select might have a combination of cells that have already had formatting applied to them and cells that do not have any formatting applied. If this is the case, you might have to click the buttons multiple times until all of the cells are formatted how you want them.

Formatting Cells Containing Numbers

Numerical data plays a central role in Excel workbooks; therefore, it stands to reason that you have lots of options for choosing how you want your numbers to appear. Two frequently used formats are the Accounting number style, which displays a cell's contents as a monetary value, and Percent, which multiplies a value by 100 and adds a percent sign to the end. The two biggest benefits of formatting data as a percent are that you save a lot of time (and avoid mistakes) by not typing the decimal point or percent sign yourself and that you can tell the values are percentages at a glance.

Two other options for formatting your numbers are to display the values in a cell with commas every third digit and to increase or decrease the number of digits to the right of the decimal point. Although two decimal places is enough for most financial data, you may need to track currency exchanges to three or four decimal places.

Display Numerical Values as Currency and Percentages

① Select the cells you want to format.

② Click the Home tab.

③ Using the tools in the Number group, follow any of these steps:

- Click the Accounting Number Format button to apply the currency style with two decimal places. You can choose a currency symbol other than your default (which is the $ sign in the United States) by clicking the down arrow at the right edge of the Accounting Number Format button.

- Click the Percent Style button to add a percent sign with no decimal places.

- Click the Comma Style button to add a comma format with two decimal places.

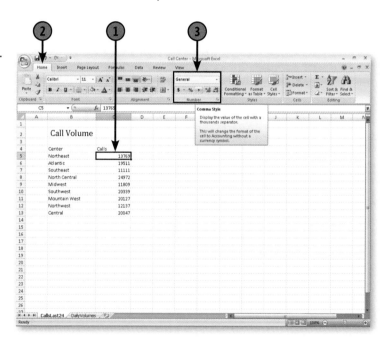

Set the Number of Decimal Places

① Select the cells you want to format.

② Click the Home tab.

③ Follow either of these steps:

■ Click the Increase Decimal button in the Number group on the ribbon.

■ Click the Decrease Decimal button in the Number group on the ribbon.

Tip

When you create a worksheet, you should apply the desired numerical formatting to all the cells in which you'll store numbers of a certain type. That way, when you type the data later (or copy it from another document), it will be formatted correctly.

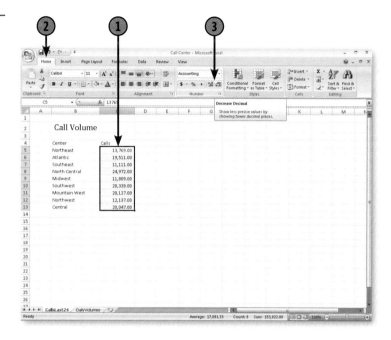

Formatting Cells Containing Dates

In many cases, knowing *when* something happened is just as important as knowing *what* happened. If you ran a garden supply store or nursery, for example, it would be useful to know that you get most of your customers on the weekends but that you make most of your large sales (most likely to landscape architects and other stores) during the week. Excel recognizes when you enter a date into a cell and applies the program's default format to the date. There are many date formats to choose from, though—pick the one you like the best!

Set a Date Format

1. Select the cells you want to format as a date.
2. Click the Home tab.
3. In the Number group, click the dialog box launcher.
4. Click the Number tab.
5. Click Date.
6. Click the date format you want.
7. Click OK.

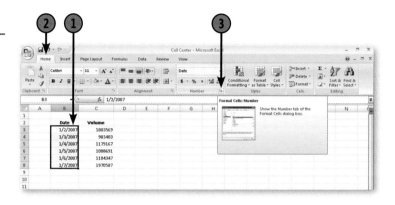

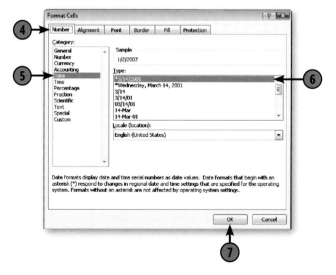

Adding Cell Backgrounds and Shading

Sometimes creating or applying a workbook theme is too much work. If all you want to do is highlight the value in a cell by changing the cell's background to red, you shouldn't go to the trouble of finding the theme that includes red as one of its colors. Instead, you can simply change the background color of cells to make those cells stand out. Be sure there's enough contrast between the background and text colors, however. Very little is worse than having to squint at the monitor to read text that blends in with the background color.

Add Background Color

(1) Select the cells you want to change.

(2) Click the Home tab.

(3) In the Font group, click the Fill Color down arrow.

(4) Select the background color you want.

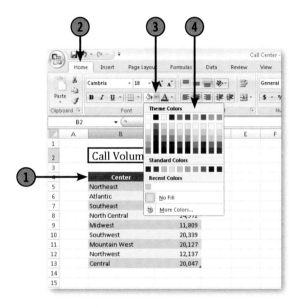

Change Background Shading

① Select the cells you want to change.

② Right-click the selection and click Format Cells from the shortcut menu.

③ Click the Fill tab.

④ Click the Pattern Color down arrow and then select the color you want.

⑤ Click the Pattern Style down arrow and then select the pattern you want.

⑥ Click OK.

Caution

If you select a set of cells, Excel applies the border you select to the entire selection. Selecting cells A2 and B2 and choosing Thick Bottom Border, therefore, would place a thick border on the bottom edge of cell B2, not on the bottom edges of cells A2 and B2.

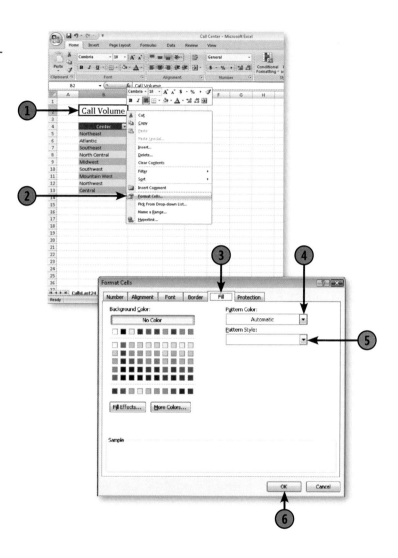

Formatting Cell Borders

The grid that appears on the standard worksheet uses light gray lines to mark cell boundaries, but those boundary lines don't distinguish one area of the worksheet from another. One way you can make a group of cells stand out from other groups is to draw a border on the edge of the cells. You can also change the color of any border you add to your worksheet.

Draw Borders

1. Select the cells around which you want to draw a border.

2. Click the Home tab.

3. Click the Border button's down arrow.

4. Click the type of border you want to apply.

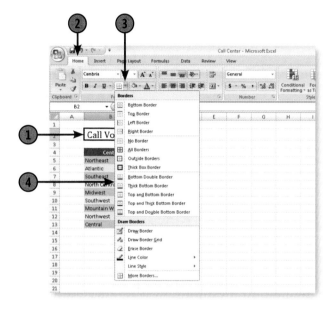

Format Cell Borders

① Click the cell you want to format.

② Click the Home tab.

③ Click the Font group's dialog box launcher.

④ Click the Border tab.

⑤ Select the line style.

⑥ Click the Color down arrow.

⑦ Click the color you want to use for the borders.

⑧ Select the borders you want to use.

⑨ Click OK.

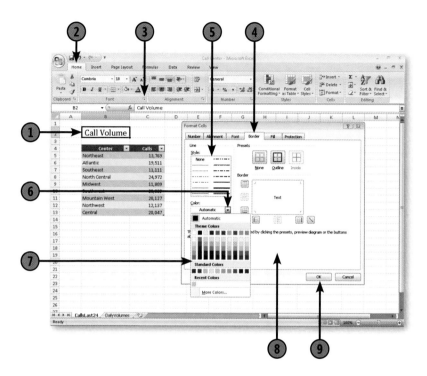

Defining Cell Styles

When you develop a worksheet, you will probably create a set of formats you want to apply consistently to certain parts of it. For example, you might always want your column headings to be slightly larger and in a different font than the body of the worksheet. You can save the formatting you want for a work- sheet element and save it as a *style*, which you then can apply to appropriate parts of your worksheets. Excel 2007 makes using styles much easier than in previous versions. Not only do you have more built-in styles from which to choose, it's no trouble to create a custom style of your own.

Apply a Style

① Select the cells you want to change.

② Click the Home tab.

③ In the Styles group, click Cell Styles.

④ Click a style.

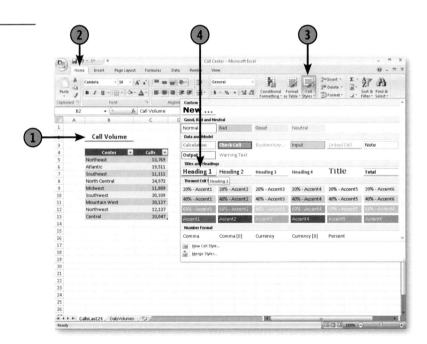

Tip

When you hover the mouse pointer over a style, the selected cells change their appearance to preview how the cells would appear if you applied that style.

Create a Style

1. Click the Home tab.

2. In the Styles group on the ribbon, click Cell Styles.

3. Click New Cell Style.

4. Type a new style name.

5. Click Format.

6. Specify the formatting you want this style to contain.

7. Click OK.

8. Click OK.

Tip

If you want to immediately apply a new style after creating it, select the cells first, create your style, and then click OK instead of Close.

Tip

Any custom styles you create will appear at the top of the Cell Styles gallery.

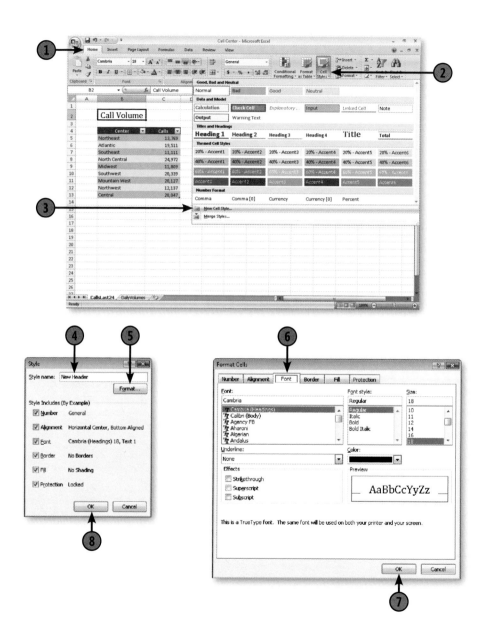

Modify a Style

① Click the Home tab.

② In the Styles group on the ribbon, click Cell Styles.

③ Right-click the style you want to modify.

④ Click Modify.

⑤ Click Format.

⑥ Specify the formatting you want.

⑦ Click OK twice.

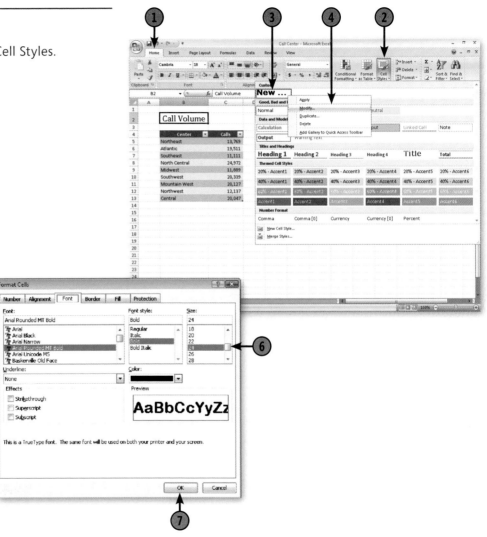

Delete a Style

① Click the Home tab.

② In the Styles group on the ribbon, click Cell Styles.

③ Right-click the style you want to delete.

④ Click Delete.

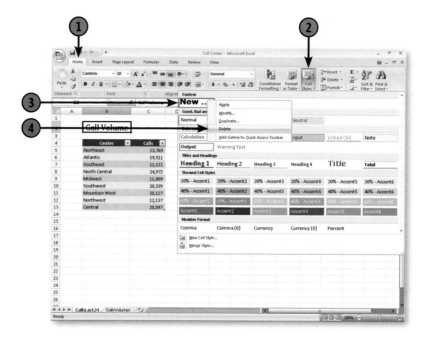

Aligning and Orienting Cell Contents

Most of the time you will want your text to be square with the left edge of a cell, but headings are much easier to read (and stand out better) when they're centered in a cell, and numbers are easier to read when the last digit of every number is flush with the right edge of a column. Similarly, if you want to create a tall, thin cell with text written in a vertical line, you can do so by typing your text into a cell and then changing the contents' orientation. When your data doesn't fit neatly into the width of a cell, you can choose to have the text displayed on a new line in the same cell. This setting, called text *wrapping*, treats a cell like a small text box with narrow margins.

Change Text Alignment

① Select the cells you want to align.

② Click the Home tab.

③ Using the controls in the Alignment group on the ribbon, follow one of these steps:

■ Click the Align Left button to align the text with the left edge of the cell.

■ Click the Center button to center the text within the cell.

■ Click the Align Right button to align the text with the right edge of the cell.

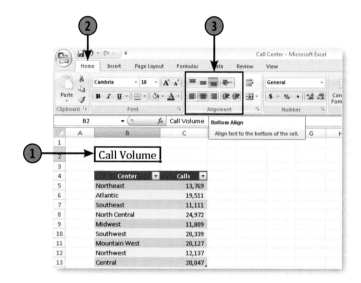

Set Text Orientation and Wrapping

① Select the cells you want to orient.

② Click the Home tab.

③ Using the controls in the Alignment group on the ribbon, follow either or both of these steps:

- ■ Click the Orientation button and select the desired orientation of your cell text.

- ■ Click the Wrap Text button to wrap the text to fit inside the column width.

Tip

If you would like more control over how to rotate the text within a cell, right-click the cells you want to orient and choose Format Cells from the shortcut menu. In the Format Cells dialog box, click the Alignment tab, and then type the number of degrees you want to rotate the baseline of your text and click OK.

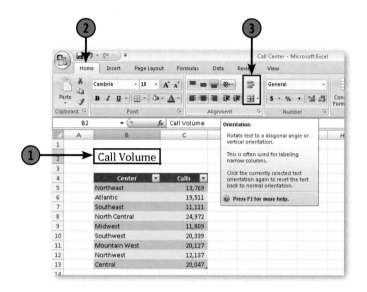

Formatting a Cell Based on Conditions

Another way you can make your data easier to interpret is to change the appearance of your data based on the value in a cell. This kind of formatting is called *conditional formatting* because the data must meet certain conditions to have a format applied to it. For example, if you use a worksheet to track your customers' credit lines, you could have a customer's outstanding balance appear in red if they are within 10 percent of their credit limit.

Excel 2007 improves upon the conditional formatting capabilities of previous versions by enabling you to create an unlimited number of conditions (you were previously limited to three), allowing more than one condition to be applied to a cell, and making it easier for you to manage your conditions.

Change the Format of a Cell Based on Its Value

1. Select the cells you want to change.

2. Click the Home tab.

3. In the Styles group on the ribbon, click Conditional Formatting.

4. Click New Rule.

5. Click Format Only Cells That Contain.

6. Click the Comparison Phrase down arrow.

7. Click the comparison phrase you want.

8. Type the constant values or formulas you want evaluated.

9. Click Format.

10. Specify the formatting you want and click OK.

11. Click OK.

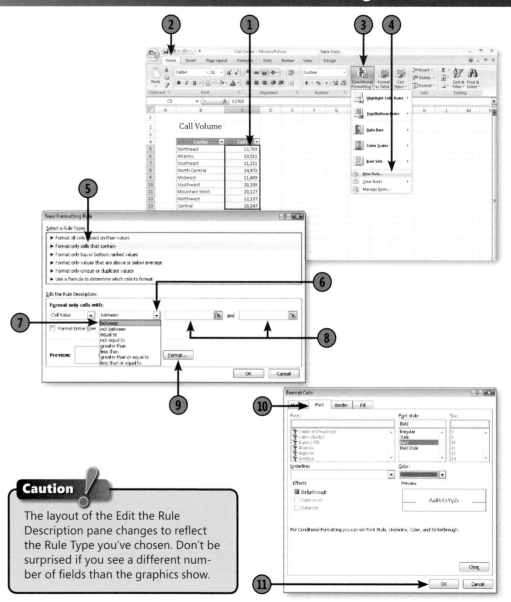

Caution

The layout of the Edit the Rule Description pane changes to reflect the Rule Type you've chosen. Don't be surprised if you see a different number of fields than the graphics show.

Change the Format of a Cell Based on the Results of a Formula

1. Select the cells you want to change.

2. Click the Home tab.

3. In the Styles group on the ribbon, click Conditional Formatting.

4. Click New Rule.

5. Click Use a formula to determine which cells to format.

6. Type the formula you want evaluated.

7. Click Format.

8. Specify the formatting you want and click OK.

9. Click OK.

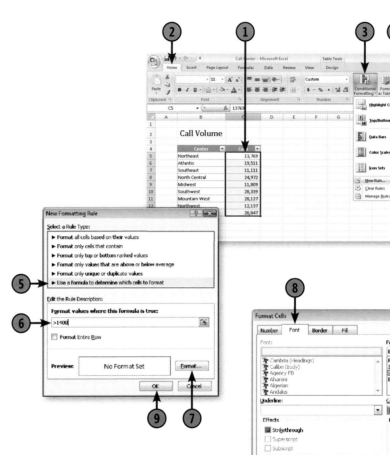

Try This!

In a blank worksheet, click cell A1, click the Home tab, click the Conditional Formatting button, and then click New Rule. Define a condition that applies when a Cell Value Is Between 400 and 1000. Apply bold formatting to the cells. Click OK. Define a second condition that applies when a Cell Value Is Less Than 400. Apply italic formatting to the cells. Click OK. Type 450 in cell A1 and press Enter. The cell's contents will be displayed in bold type. Click cell A1, type 350, and press Enter. The cell's contents will now be displayed in italics.

Edit a Conditional Formatting Rule

1. Select the cells that contain the rule you want to edit.

2. Click the Home tab.

3. In the Styles group, click Conditional Formatting.

4. Click Manage Rules.

5. Click the rule you want to change.

6. Click Edit Rule.

7. Use the controls to make your changes.

8. Click OK twice to save your changes.

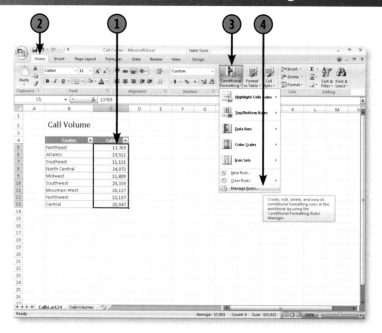

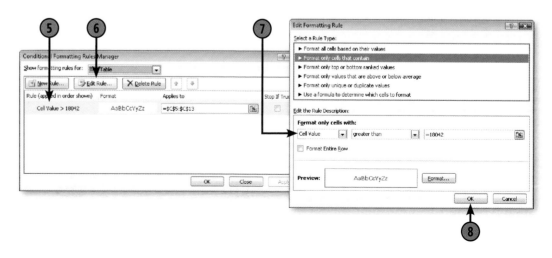

Delete a Conditional Formatting Rule

① Select the cells that contain the rule you want to edit.

② Click the Home tab.

③ In the Styles group, click Conditional Formatting.

④ Click Manage Rules.

⑤ Click the rule you want to delete.

⑥ Click Delete Rule.

⑦ Click OK.

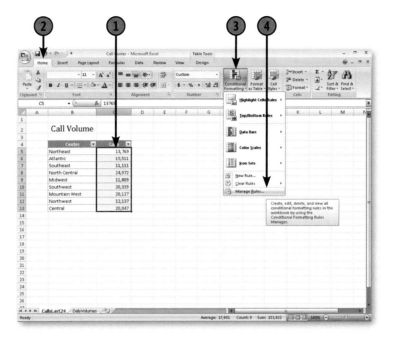

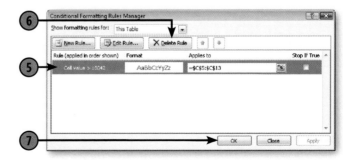

Changing How Conditional Formatting Rules Are Applied

Excel 2007 enables you to create more powerful conditional formatting rules, but that's not the only new trick in your conditional formatting bag. In prior versions of the program, when Excel found a condition that applied to your cell data, it stopped checking. That meant if you had one rule that formatted values of more than 1000 as bold text and another that formatted values of more than 1500 as italic text, the value 1600 would be formatted according only to the first rule applied.

In Excel 2007, you can decide whether Excel should stop after it finds a rule that applies to your data or continue to check other rules. You can also change the order in which Excel checks your conditions to control how Excel applies the rules. Rule order only matters if you choose to have Excel stop after it applies a rule.

Stop when a Condition Is Met

① Select the cells that contain the rule you want to edit.

② Click the Home tab.

③ In the Styles group, click Conditional Formatting.

④ Click Manage Rules.

⑤ Click the rule you want to change.

⑥ Select the Stop If True box.

⑦ Click OK.

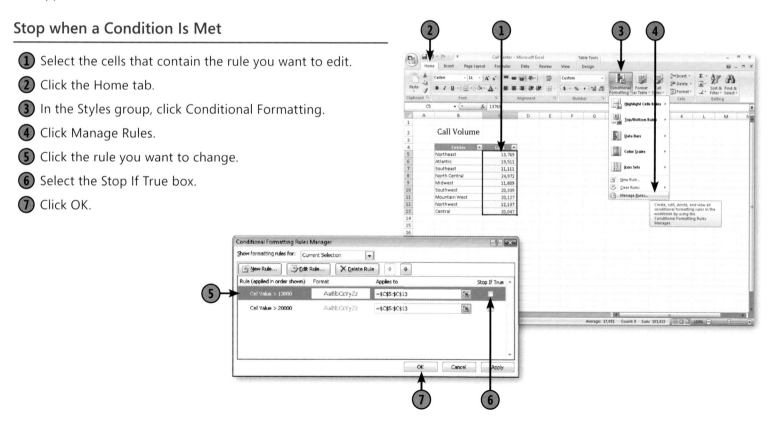

Change the Order of Conditions

① Select the cells that contain the rules you want to edit.

② Click the Home tab.

③ In the Styles group, click Conditional Formatting.

④ Click Manage Rules.

⑤ Click the rule you want to change.

⑥ Follow either of these steps:

■ Click the Move Up button to move the rule one place higher in the order.

■ Click the Move Down button to move the rule one place lower in the order.

⑦ Click OK.

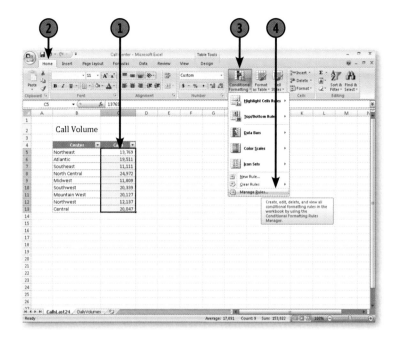

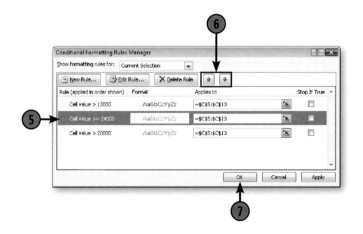

Displaying Data Bars, Icon Sets, or Color Scales Based on Cell Values

Organizations of all kinds track their performance data in Microsoft Excel. The specific numbers are important, of course, but it's also important that you be able to tell how the numbers relate to each other and whether your department is meeting its performance goals. Color scales and data bars show how the data in a cell compares to other data in the selected range. The higher a value is in relation to the other values in the range, the longer the data bar or the more the color is toward the high end of the scale. Icon sets, by contrast, test a value to see whether it is in the top, middle, or bottom third of the values in the range. You can change the tests to determine which icon or color is shown when.

Display Data Bars

1. Select the cells that contain your data.

2. Click the Home tab.

3. In the Styles group on the ribbon, click Conditional Formatting.

4. Point to Data Bars.

5. Click the data bar option you want to apply.

Display Icon Sets

1. Select the cells that contain your data.

2. Click the Home tab.

3. In the Styles group on the ribbon, click Conditional Formatting.

4. Point to Icon Sets.

5. Click the icon set you want to apply.

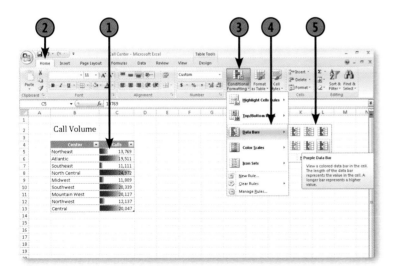

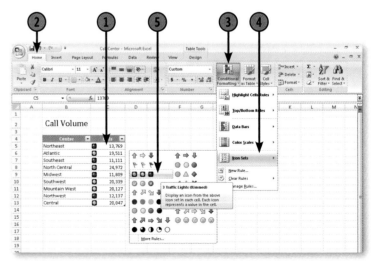

Display Color Scales

1. Select the cells that contain your data.

2. Click the Home tab.

3. In the Styles group on the ribbon, click Conditional Formatting.

4. Point to Color Scales.

5. Click the color scale pattern you want to apply.

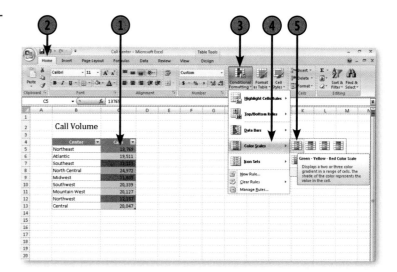

Tip

When you click Data Bars, Icon Sets, or Color Scales, you'll see an item named More Rules at the bottom of the gallery of built-in formats. Clicking More Rules displays a dialog box you can use to control the format's details.

Copying Formats with the Format Painter

After you create a format for a cell or group of cells, you can copy the format from one group of cells to another group of cells using the Format Painter. The Format Painter lets you copy the format quickly, saving you the time and effort it would take to copy the contents of another cell with the desired format and then change the data or formula.

Copy Styles with the Format Painter

1. Select the cells with the formatting you want to copy.

2. Click the Home tab.

3. In the Clipboard group, click the Format Painter button.

4. Select the cells where you want the formatting applied.

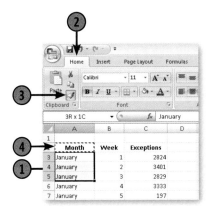

Merging or Splitting Cells or Data

You can change a row's height or a column's width, but this might not be the best way to improve your worksheet's usability. For instance, a label might not fit within a single cell, and increasing that cell's width, or every cell's width, might throw off the worksheet's design. One solution to this problem is to merge two or more cells. Merging cells allows you to treat a group of cells as a single cell as far as content and formatting go.

Merge Several Cells into One

① Select the cells you want to merge.

② Click the Home tab.

③ In the Alignment group, click the Merge And Center button.

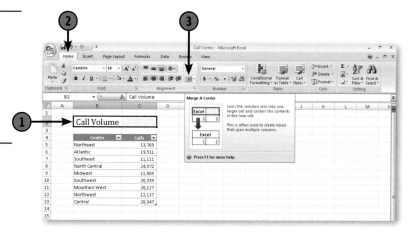

Split a Merged Cell

■ Click the merged cell.

■ Click the Home tab.

■ Click the down arrow at the right edge of the Merge And Center button.

■ Click Split Cells.

Caution

If the cells you selected have data in more than one cell, only the data in the upper-left cell will remain after you merge the cells.

Tip

If you do not want the merged data centered, click a different alignment from the Alignment group on the Home tab.

8

Formatting the Worksheet

Microsoft Office Excel 2007 enables you to change your worksheets' appearance and structure to display your data effectively. For example, you can make rows and columns surrounding your data wider so your figures are separated from the worksheet's other contents. You can also move entire rows or columns to different locations in the workbook, such as when a worksheet's data columns are in a different order than those of a related paper form. If you want to call attention to one of your worksheets, perhaps one that contains new data your boss should review, you can change the color of that worksheet's sheet tab so that it stands out within the workbook.

Applying Workbook Themes

Designing attractive Excel worksheets challenges even the most advanced users. Prior to Excel 2007, you could only format your worksheets quickly by using a series of not-very-inspiring AutoFormats. Excel 2007, by contrast, comes with a wide variety of attractive themes that you can apply to your worksheets. But you're not limited to the themes included when you install Excel! You can create your own themes, find many more themes on the Microsoft Office Templates Web site, and trade themed workbooks with other users.

Apply a Workbook Theme

1. Click the Page Layout tab.

2. In the Themes group on the ribbon, click Themes.

3. Click the theme you want to apply.

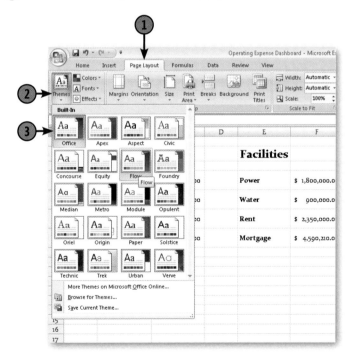

Change Colors within a Theme

1. Click the Page Layout tab.

2. In the Themes group on the ribbon, click Colors.

3. Click the color scheme you want to apply.

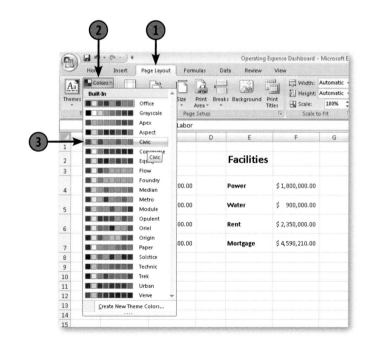

Change Fonts within a Theme

1. Click the Page Layout tab.

2. In the Themes group on the ribbon, click Fonts.

3. Click the font scheme you want to apply.

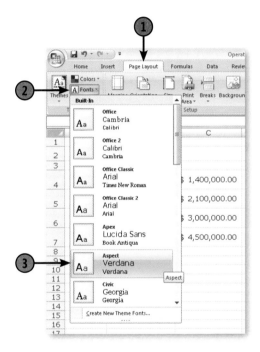

Change Effects within a Theme

1. Click the Page Layout tab.

2. In the Themes group on the ribbon, click Effects.

3. Click the effects scheme you want to apply.

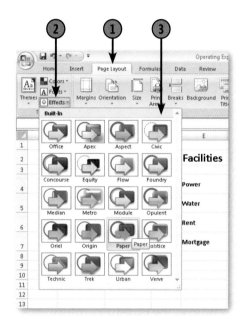

Create a New Workbook Theme

1. Format your worksheet using the colors, fonts, and effects you want to include in your theme.

2. Click the Page Layout tab.

3. In the Themes group on the ribbon, click Themes.

4. Click Save Current Theme.

5. Type a name for your theme.

6. Click Save.

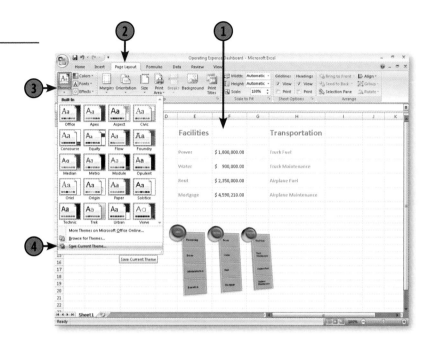

> **Tip**
>
> You can find a collection of existing themes and themed documents on the Microsoft Office Online: Templates home page. To display that Web page, click the Page Layout tab, click Themes, and then click Search Office Online.

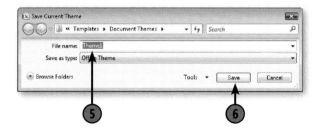

Coloring Sheet Tabs

A great way to make any worksheet element stand out is to change it to a color that contrasts with the other colors used in the worksheet. In Excel 2007, you can change the color of sheet tabs. For example, you can change the color of a sheet tab in a workbook in which you track sales for a year, with a worksheet for each month. Rather than move the current worksheet to the front of the list, which would put the worksheets out of order, you can change the color of the sheet tab to make it stand out. When the month ends, you can remove the color from that sheet tab and apply it to the new month's sheet tab.

Color a Sheet Tab

① Hold down the Ctrl key and click the sheet tabs you want to color.

② Right-click the selection and point to Tab Color on the shortcut menu.

③ Click the color you want.

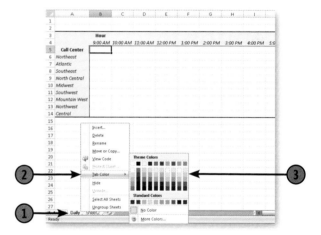

Tip

If you select a sheet tab color from the Theme Colors section of the color palette, changing your workbook's theme will change your sheet tabs' colors.

Changing a Worksheet's Gridlines

Gridlines are the lines on your worksheets that define the cells formed by the intersections of rows and columns. The default gridline color is gray, and not all worksheets work well with this standard setting. Sometimes you'll want to change the color of the cell gridlines or even turn them off. Excel 2007 also makes it easier than in previous editions to control whether your gridlines appear when you print a worksheet.

Change the Color of Cell Gridlines

1. Click the Microsoft Office button.

2. Click Excel Options.

3. Click Advanced.

4. Click the Display Options for this Worksheet down arrow.

5. Select the worksheet, or workbook, to which you want to apply the change.

6. Click the Gridline Color button.

7. Select the color you want to use for the gridlines.

8. Click OK.

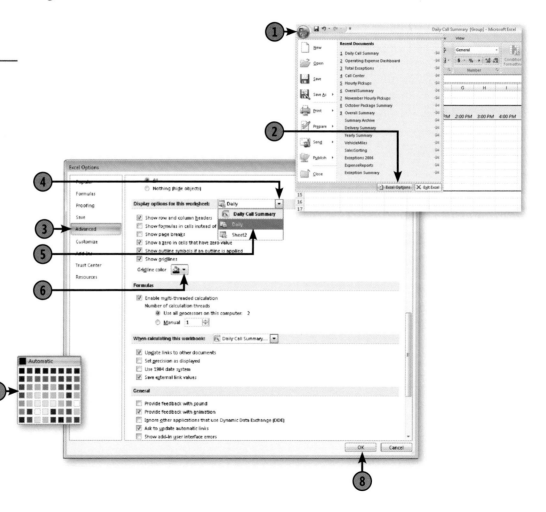

Show or Hide Cell Gridlines

① Click the Page Layout tab.

② Using the controls in the Sheet Options group on the ribbon, follow either or both of these steps using the check boxes in the Gridlines section of the group:

- Select the View check box to show the gridlines as you work in Excel or clear the View check box to hide the gridlines as you work.

- Select the Print check box to show the gridlines when you print the worksheet or clear the Print check box to hide the gridlines when you print.

Changing Row Heights and Column Widths

When you create an Excel workbook, the default worksheet rows are tall enough to accommodate text and numbers entered in the standard character format (Calibri, 11 point) and wide enough to display about eight characters. If your text takes up too much space to fit in the cell (because you've changed the font size for a column label, for example), you can widen the column so that the contents of every cell can be seen. You can also increase the height of rows in your worksheet to put some space between values, which will make your data easier to read. If a column is too wide or a row is too high, you can make it narrower or shorter, as needed.

Resize a Row

① Hover the mouse pointer over the lower boundary of the row you want to resize until the mouse pointer turns into a two-headed arrow.

② Drag the boundary until the row is the height you want.

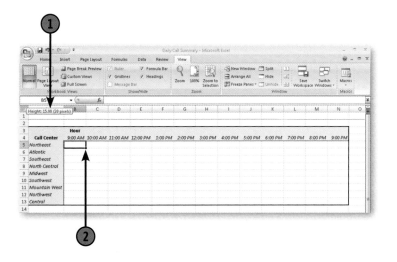

Resize a Column

① Hover the mouse pointer over the right boundary of the column you want to resize until the mouse pointer turns into a two-headed arrow.

② Drag the boundary until the column is the width you want.

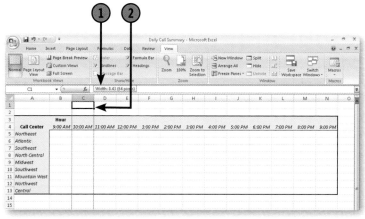

Tip

You can resize a column to fit the text of its widest cell by double-clicking the right boundary of the column.

Resizing Multiple Rows or Columns

1 Select the rows or columns you want to resize.

2 Drag the border of any selected column or row to the desired width or height.

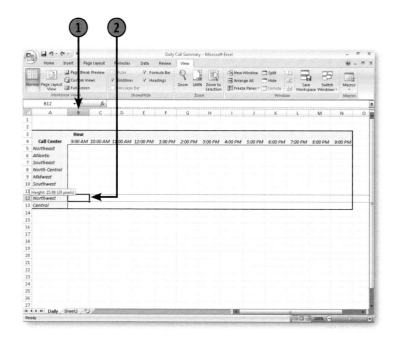

Inserting Rows or Columns

After you've created a worksheet and begun filling in your data, you might decide to insert a row or column to add data you didn't think to include when you started. For example, a customer might want to add a product to an order. To accommodate this, you can insert a blank row below the last row in the existing order and add the new item there. If you wanted to add a row in the middle of the existing order data, you could insert a blank row above an existing row. You can perform similar actions with columns: If you want to begin recording a new piece of information about your customers, such as a Web site or e-mail address, you can add a column to store that information. You can even use the Insert Options smart tag to format the new rows or columns.

Insert a Row in a Worksheet

1. Right-click the row header below where you want the new row to appear.

2. Choose Insert from the shortcut menu.

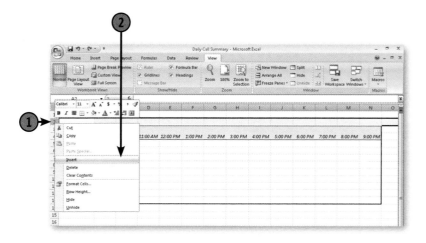

Insert a Column in a Worksheet

1 Right-click the column header to the right of where you want the new column to appear.

2 Choose Insert from the shortcut menu.

Set Insert Options

1 After inserting rows or columns, click the Insert Options smart tag.

2 Select the type of formatting you want the new cells to have.

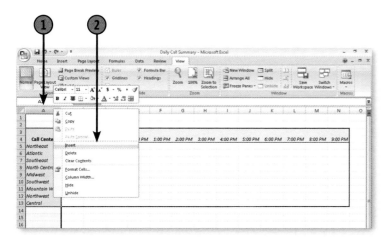

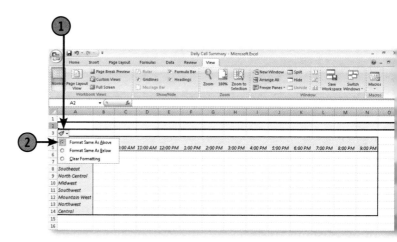

Tip

If you want to insert more than one row or column at a time, select a number of existing rows or columns equal to the number you want to insert and then choose the Insert command from the shortcut menu.

Tip

The Insert Options smart tag will appear only if the cells above or below the insertion point have special formatting.

Moving Rows and Columns

In many cases, the data in your worksheets will have first been recorded on paper—for example, when you record times for a race or collect customer responses on survey forms. Sometimes it's easier to type the information into your worksheet so that it looks the same way as it looked on paper. You can move rows and columns to new positions on the worksheet in order to present the information the way you want it to look.

Move One or More Rows

1 Select the rows you want to move.

2 Click the Home tab.

3 In the Clipboard group, click the Cut button.

4 Click the first cell in the row where you want the rows to be moved.

5 In the Clipboard group, click the Paste button.

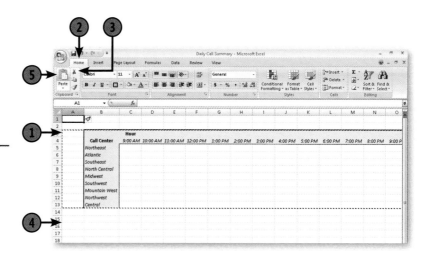

Move One or More Columns

1 Select the columns you want to move.

2 Click the Home tab.

3 In the Clipboard group, click the Cut button.

4 Click the first cell in the column where you want to move the columns.

5 In the Clipboard group, click the Paste button.

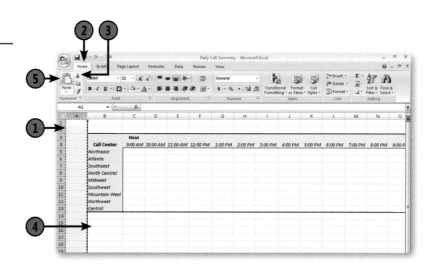

Deleting Rows and Columns

Excel workbooks are a great place to store and manipulate your data, but there might be times when you no longer need to use a particular row or column. Whether you placed an extra column to add some white space between the main body of data and a summary calculation, or a row holds the contact information of a customer who has asked to be removed from your list, you can delete a row or column quickly and easily.

Delete a Row or Column

(1) Select the row or column you want to delete.

(2) Right-click the selection and choose Delete from the shortcut menu.

Caution

Formulas that reference cells in the columns or rows you delete will no longer work. The Error smart tag will tell you that there is an Invalid Cell Reference Error and give you options to fix the problem. #REF will appear in the damaged cell.

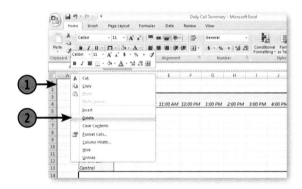

Outlining to Hide and Show Rows and Columns

When you develop worksheets, you'll probably try to keep similar entries together. For example, if you create a worksheet that lists all of the products you sell, you can group the products by category. In the case of a garden supply store, all of the tools would be together, then the furniture, and then a new category for each type of plant. If you want to hide the rows for one set of products, you can define the rows as a group, and you'll then have the option to choose which rows you would like displayed. The rows you hide are only gone temporarily. The data hasn't been deleted, it's just been moved out of your way while you don't need it.

Group Rows and Columns

① Select the rows or columns you want to group.

② Click the Data tab.

③ In the Outline group on the ribbon, click Group.

④ In the dialog box that appears, verify that the Rows or Columns option button (as appropriate) is selected, and then click OK.

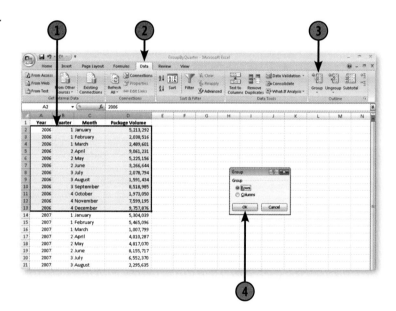

Ungroup Rows and Columns

1. Select the rows or columns you want to ungroup.

2. Click the Data tab.

3. In the Outline group on the ribbon, click Ungroup.

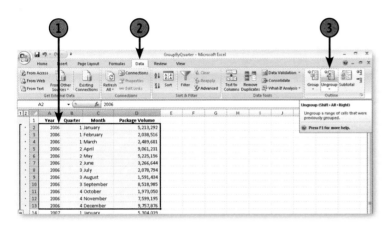

Hide Grouped Rows and Columns

1. Click the Collapse button next to the group you want to hide.

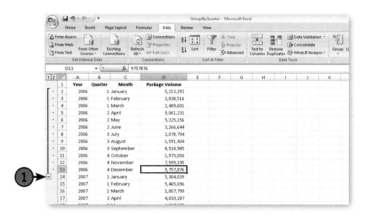

Show Grouped Rows and Columns

1. Click the Expand button next to the group you want to show.

 See Also

For information about calculating subtotals for groups of rows, see "Summing with Subtotals and Grand Totals" on page 89.

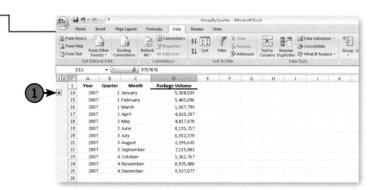

Hiding Rows and Columns

If you're working with a worksheet that contains lots of data, you might need to refer to the contents of rows or columns that aren't close enough on the worksheet to appear on the same screen. Rather than scrolling back and forth to access the data you need, you can hide any intervening rows or columns so everything you need to see is displayed on the screen at the same time. The rows you hide are only gone temporarily; the data hasn't been deleted; it's just been moved out of your way while you don't need it.

Hide Rows or Columns

1. Select the rows or columns you want to hide.

2. Right-click the selection and choose Hide from the shortcut menu.

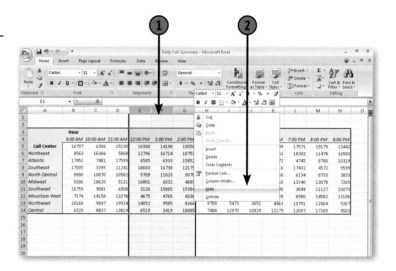

Tip

You can tell that there are hidden rows or columns in a worksheet in two ways. First, whenever rows or columns are hidden, row numbers or column letters will be missing. For example, if rows 2 through 4 are hidden, the first two visible rows of the worksheet will be labeled row 1 and row 5.

The other way you can tell that a worksheet contains hidden rows or columns is that a thick line will appear on the border of the row header or column header where the rows or columns would otherwise appear.

Unhide Rows or Columns

1. Click the row or column header of the row above or to the left of the rows or columns you want to unhide.

2. Select the rows or columns that surround the rows or columns you want to unhide.

3. Right-click the selection and choose Unhide from the shortcut menu.

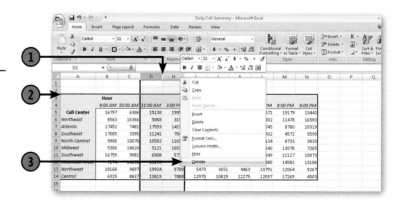

Protecting Worksheets from Changes

When you create a worksheet that contains sensitive data or data you don't want changed by anyone other than yourself, you can protect the worksheet from unauthorized changes. From within the Protect Sheet dialog box, you can choose the actions you want to allow all users to be able to perform on the worksheet. The options selected by default will allow anyone to select a cell but will prevent them from deleting rows or columns, changing any formatting, or editing scenarios attached to the worksheet.

Protect a Worksheet

1. Click the Review tab.

2. Click Protect Sheet.

3. Select the protection options you want.

4. Click OK.

Tip

Specify a password in the Protect Sheet dialog box to restrict access to a workbook, worksheet, or part of a worksheet. After you've done this, only authorized users will be able to make changes.

Tip

You can protect chart sheets and other graphic objects in worksheets from unauthorized changes. Keep in mind, however, that if the source data for a chart sheet changes, your chart sheet will also change, even if you have the chart protected.

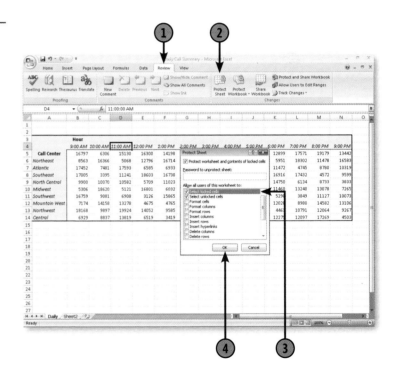

Locking Cells to Prevent Changes

After you protect a worksheet, you can lock an individual cell to prevent it from being changed. This level of protection goes beyond simply protecting a worksheet; it prevents anyone using the worksheet from changing the contents or formatting of the cell. Excel 2007 enables this option by default.

Lock Cells

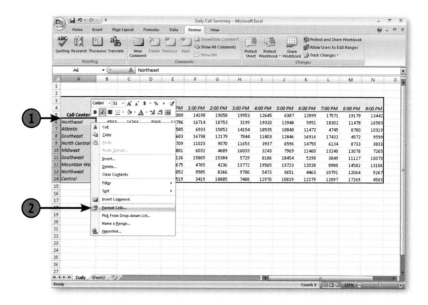

① Select the cells you want to lock.

② Right-click the selection and click Format Cells on the shortcut menu.

③ Click the Protection tab.

④ Select the Locked check box.

⑤ Click OK.

Caution

You must protect your worksheet after you lock the cells for your locked cells to become effective.

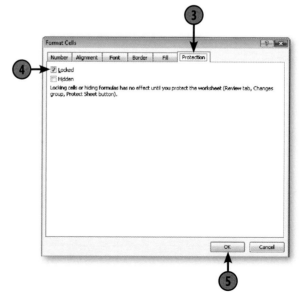

9

Printing Worksheets

After you have created your worksheet, you can print a copy for reference, backup, or to distribute to your colleagues. Although you might be tempted to print your worksheet as soon as you have completed it, it's usually a good idea to check your work first. All you need to see how your worksheet will look when printed is to display the worksheet in Print Preview mode. If you want to change how your worksheet will appear on the printed page, you can do anything from changing the orientation of the printout (that is, printing in a vertical format, called portrait mode or a horizontal format, called landscape mode) to scaling the worksheet to fit within a specific number of pages. It's easy to fine-tune margins, adjust headers and footers, and customize a variety of other print options as well.

Previewing Worksheets Before Printing

Before you print a worksheet, it's helpful to take a step back and look at how your data will appear on the printed page. To do that in Excel, you display your worksheet in Print Preview mode. While you have your workbook open in Print Preview, you can zoom in to see cell contents clearly without altering printing size. You can also adjust the widths of any columns in Print Preview, saving you the trouble of switching between Print Preview and the standard Excel window. Excel 2007 also enables you to view your workbook in Page Layout View, which displays your workbook as it will be printed while still enabling you to edit the workbook's contents easily.

Display a Worksheet in Page Layout View

① Click the View tab.

② In the Workbook Views group, click Page Layout View.

View and Zoom Worksheets in Print Preview

① Click the Microsoft Office button.

② Click the Print item's right arrow.

③ Click Print Preview.

(continued on the next page)

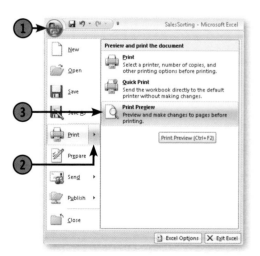

View and Zoom Worksheets
in Print Preview *(continued)*

4 Click any area of the worksheet
to switch between magnified and
full-page view.

5 Click Close Print Preview.

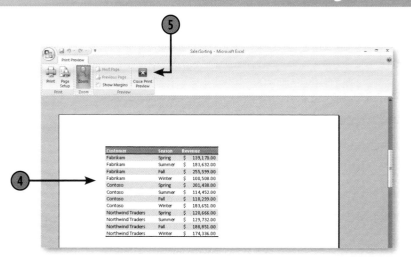

Change Column Widths
and Row Heights in Page
Layout View

1 Click the View tab.

2 Click Page Layout View.

3 Hover the mouse pointer over the
edge of a column or row header
until the mouse pointer becomes
a two-headed arrow. Drag the
edge until the column or row is
the desired size.

4 Click Normal to return to
Normal view.

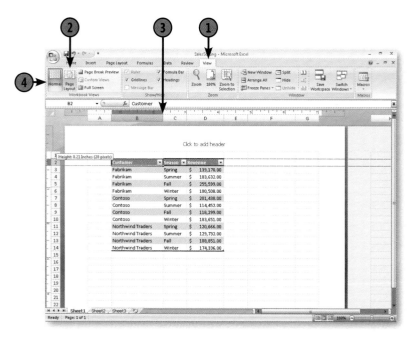

Printing Worksheets with Current Options

After you've entered all of your data and formatted your worksheets so the data is easy to read, you can print your worksheets for distribution to your colleagues, for example. Opening the File menu, pointing to Print, and clicking Quick Print prints only the worksheet displayed on the screen—if you want to print more than one worksheet at a time, such as when you want to print out several months of sales results and each month is recorded on a separate worksheet, you can do that as well.

Print Multiple Worksheets from the Same Workbook

① Hold down the Ctrl key and click the sheet tabs of the worksheets you want to print.

② Click the Microsoft Office button.

③ Point to Print.

④ Click Quick Print.

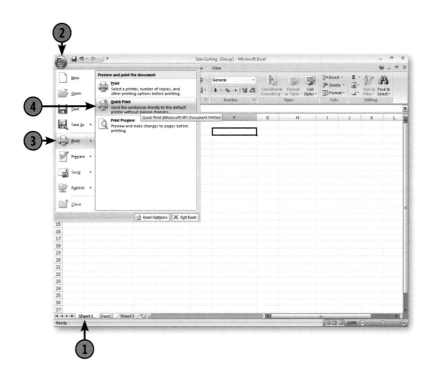

Tip

If all of the worksheets in a workbook are adjacent, click the sheet tab for the first worksheet, hold down the Shift key, and click the sheet tab for the last worksheet. Click the Quick Print button on the Quick Access Toolbar to print all of the selected worksheets.

Caution

If you drag a column marker so far to the left that you overlap with or pass over another column marker, the column you are adjusting will be hidden from view.

Choosing Whether to Print Gridlines and Headings

Excel is a spreadsheet program, which means that it generally expects the data you enter into it to be organized into rows and columns. You're not limited to entering just rows and columns of dry figures, of course; you can add images, place text in cells outside of your tables, and format your worksheet so your data looks exactly the way you want it to.

In the spirit of offering you as much control as possible, Excel enables you to choose whether you print your worksheets' gridlines, column headings, and row headings. If you've

printed any Microsoft Office documents, you've probably noticed that some elements that work very well on your computer screen don't translate well to the printed page. Gridlines, column headings, and row headings are like that. When you're looking at data on a computer screen, those three elements usually help you make sense of your data, but those same elements will often clutter your printouts. It's up to you, however; you can choose to print your headings and gridlines or not.

Choose to Print Gridlines

① Click the Page Layout tab.

② In the Sheet Options group, under Gridlines, select the Print check box.

Choose to Print Headings

① Click the Page Layout tab.

② In the Sheet Options group, under Headings, select the Print check box.

Choosing Printers and Paper Options

You might not want to use the same printer and paper type for everything you print. Standard 8.5-by-11-inch letter size paper will be fine for printing some of your worksheets, but from time to time, you'll probably need to use 8.5-by-14-inch legal size paper. You can also choose from a variety of media options that include materials other than the standard type of paper you would find in most homes and offices. For example, you might want to print on coated paper, transparencies, envelopes, or even T-shirt transfer paper.

Choose a Printer

1. Click the Microsoft Office button.
2. Click Print.
3. Click the Name down arrow.
4. Click the printer you want to use.
5. Click OK.

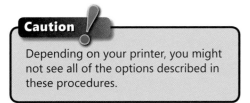

Caution

Depending on your printer, you might not see all of the options described in these procedures.

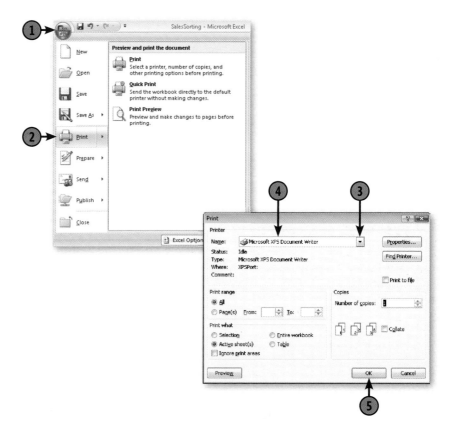

Choose the Paper

① Click the Microsoft Office button.

② Click Print.

③ Click Properties.

④ Click the Paper/Quality tab.

⑤ Click the Document Size down arrow.

⑥ Select the paper size.

⑦ Click the Paper Type down arrow.

⑧ Click the type of paper you want.

⑨ Click OK.

Caution

If you change the print media for one worksheet, the change is only effective for that worksheet.

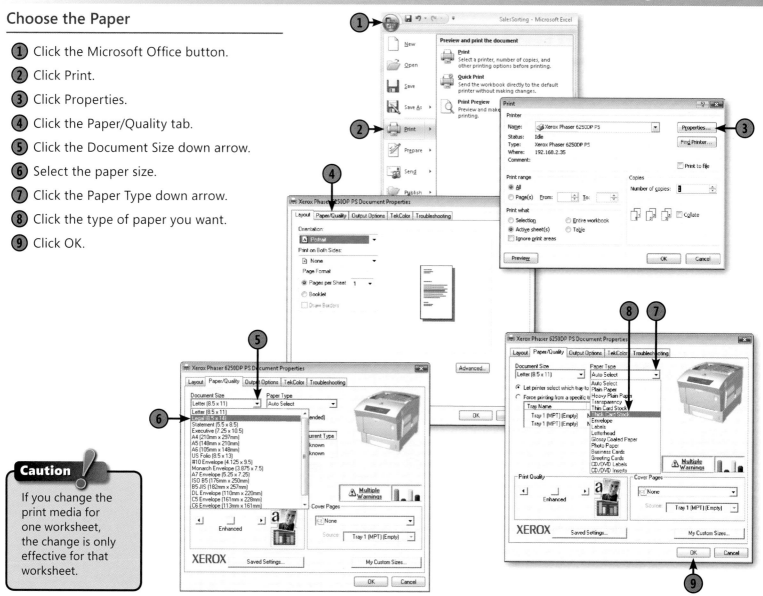

Printing Part of a Worksheet

When you create a worksheet containing lots of data, you might want to print the section of the worksheet with the data relevant to the point you're trying to illustrate. The good news is you can set a print area so Excel will print as much or as little of your worksheet as you like. The print area is outlined with a dashed line, so you can tell which cells will be printed and which won't. When you set a Print Area, you can select cells in a single rectangle or select cells located in various areas of your worksheet.

Set a Print Area

1. Select cells you want to print.
2. Click the Page Layout tab.
3. Click Print Area.
4. Click Set Print Area.

Remove a Print Area

- Click the Page Layout tab.
- Click Print Area.
- Click Clear Print Area.

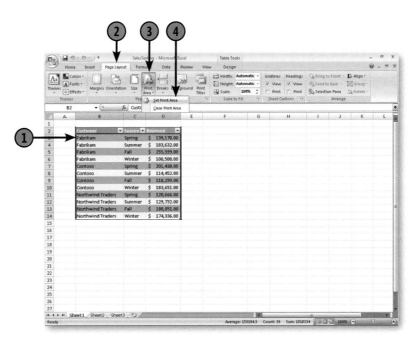

Tip

Try to arrange your data so the content to be printed looks the same on the screen as it will on the printed page. You can define print areas from multiple parts of the same worksheet, but you should keep that technique in reserve for when your worksheet data appears on more than one page.

Printing Row and Column Headings on Each Page

When you print a worksheet in which the data doesn't fit on a single screen, you might have trouble remembering which data is stored in which column. Rather than make you look back to the top of the worksheet, or even type your headings where you guess the screen transitions occur, you can have

Excel print your column and row headings at the top of every page. By printing the column and row headings on each page, you will save time, improve accuracy, and reduce frustration when dealing with large worksheets.

Identify the Rows and Columns to Repeat

① Click the Page Layout tab.

② Click Print Titles.

③ Click the Sheet tab.

④ Click in the Rows To Repeat At Top box.

⑤ On your worksheet, select the row headings you want to repeat.

⑥ Click the Columns To Repeat At Left box.

⑦ On your worksheet, select the column headings you want to repeat.

⑧ Click OK.

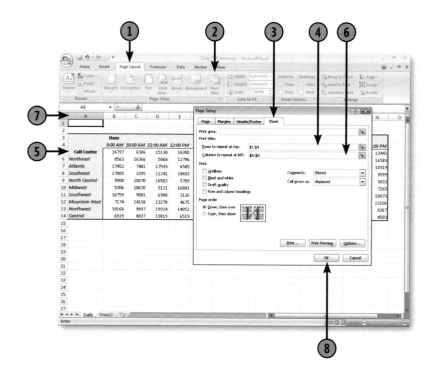

Tip

Repeating rows and columns on every page is useful when your worksheet contains frozen panes and you want to have the frozen panes appear on every page of the printout, just as they appear on the screen.

See Also

For more information about frozen panes, see "View Multiple Parts of a Worksheet by Freezing Panes" on page 76.

Setting and Changing Print Margins

Margins define the white boundary area of the page and provide a visual border around your printed data. Changing a worksheet's margins increases or decreases the amount of data displayed on a page, which allows you to make room for one last column of data, to divide your columns evenly between two pages, or to allow for enough room at one edge for the page to be bound in a report or three-ring binder. In Print Preview mode, margins appear as dark gray lines, which you can drag to the desired position.

Set Page Margins

1. Click the Page Layout tab.

2. Click Margins and either click the desired margin settings or click Custom Margins.

3. If you selected Custom Margins, type new values for the worksheet's margins in the Top, Bottom, Left, and Right boxes.

4. Click OK.

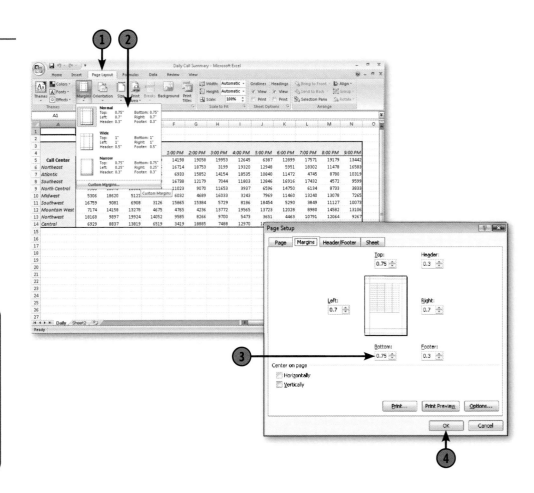

Try This!

Select multiple worksheets by holding down the Ctrl key and clicking the sheet tabs, click the Page Layout tab, click Margins, and then click Custom Margins. Type **0.75** in the Top, Bottom, Left, and Right boxes, and then click OK. All of the selected worksheets' margins will be changed to three-quarters of an inch.

Adjust Page Margins in Print Preview

① Click the Microsoft Office button.

② Click the Print item's arrow.

③ Click Print Preview.

④ If necessary, select the Show Margins check box to display the margin lines.

⑤ Hover the mouse pointer over one of the gray lines until the mouse pointer becomes a two-headed arrow. Drag the line until the margin is set the way you want.

⑥ Click Close Print Preview.

Caution

In Print Preview mode, it's sometimes difficult to distinguish between margins and header or footer lines. Be sure to keep track of which is which.

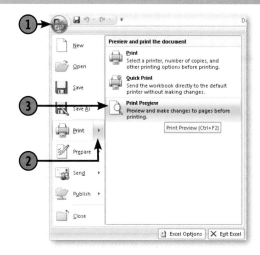

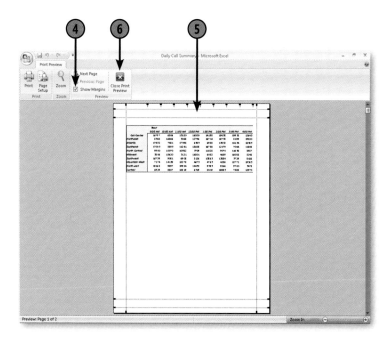

Setting Page Orientation and Scale

As you look at your worksheet and think about how you want it to appear on the printed page, be aware that you have the choice of printing in a vertical format (portrait mode) or a horizontal format (landscape mode). Landscape mode is particularly useful when you have a lot of columns in your worksheet, such as in a worksheet storing customer contact or product sales information. You can fit your worksheet onto a specific number of printed pages, which helps if you have been allotted a fixed number of pages in which to present your data in a typeset report.

Set Page Orientation

1. Click the Page Layout tab.

2. Click Orientation.

3. Select either the Portrait or Landscape option.

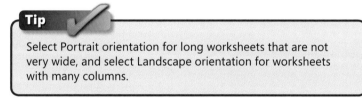

Tip

Select Portrait orientation for long worksheets that are not very wide, and select Landscape orientation for worksheets with many columns.

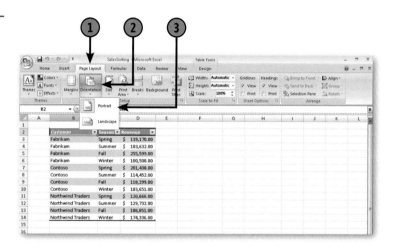

Scale the Printout to a Fixed Number of Pages

①　Click the Page Layout tab.

②　In the Scale to Fit group, click the Width down arrow and select the number of horizontal pages your worksheet should take up when printed.

③　In the Scale to Fit group, click the Height down arrow and select the number of vertical pages your worksheet should take up when printed.

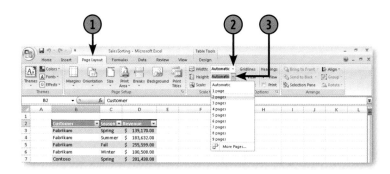

 **Tip**

Click the Microsoft Office button, click the Print item's arrow, and then click Print Preview to see how the document will look after it is forced onto a fixed number of pages.

Tip

The maximum number of pages you can choose from the Width and Height list boxes is nine. If you want to force your worksheet to print on 10 or more pages in either dimension, click the Scale to Fit dialog box launcher, select the Fit To option button, and then type how many pages the rows (pages wide) and columns (tall) should be forced to fit. Click OK.

 Try This!

Click the Page Layout tab and then click the Page Setup group's dialog box launcher. In the Page Setup dialog box, click the Page tab and then select the Fit To option. Type 1 in the Page(s) Wide box and delete the contents of the Tall box. The worksheet will now fit on a single page width but will print on additional vertical pages if necessary.

Creating Headers and Footers

Headers and footers contain information that appears at the top and bottom of each page of your printed worksheet. You can select a premade header or footer that contains information about your file, or you can create your own custom headers and footers using pre-defined text. Excel 2007 comes with a list of expressions you can insert into your headers and footers to display certain information about your worksheet, such as page numbers or file names. Headers might include helpful information such as a workbook name, and footers can include page numbers, file names, or dates.

Add a Premade Header and Footer

1. Click the Insert tab.

2. Click Header & Footer.

3. Click Header.

4. Click the premade header you want to use.

5. If desired, click Footer, and then click the premade footer you want to use.

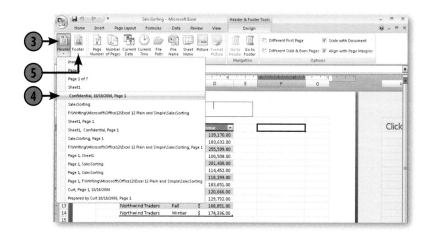

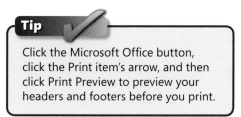

Tip

Click the Microsoft Office button, click the Print item's arrow, and then click Print Preview to preview your headers and footers before you print.

See Also

For more information about how to change the size of your headers, see "Adjust Header and Footer Height" on page 158.

Add Pre-Defined Text to the Header or Footer

1 Click the Insert tab.

2 Click Header & Footer.

3 Click the section of the header or footer where you want your text to appear and type the text you want.

4 If you want to use pre-defined text, position the insertion point where you want the text to appear.

5 Click a button to insert the pre-defined text.

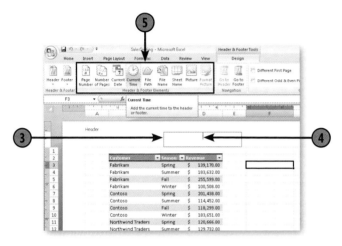

Tip

You can change the appearance of your header and footer text by selecting the text or the code representing the value to be printed (for example, the current time) and using the controls on the Home tab of the ribbon.

Adjust Header and Footer Height

1. Click the Microsoft Office button.
2. Click the Print item's arrow.
3. Click Print Preview.
4. If necessary, click Show Margins to display the header and footer lines.
5. Hover the mouse pointer over one of the gray lines until the mouse pointer becomes a two-headed arrow. Drag the line until the header or footer is the height you want.
6. Click Close Print Preview.

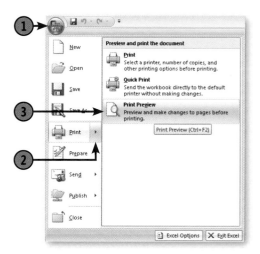

Tip

The directions of the arrowheads show you in which direction you can move the line.

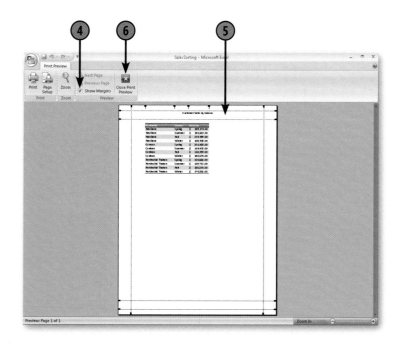

Adding Graphics to a Header or a Footer

Creating attractive and professional looking printouts will help you communicate your message better. Often, the addition of a simple graphic to a header or footer will give your worksheet a truly professional appearance. You might want to create printouts that include your company's letterhead or logo or a graphic related to the information on your worksheet. An excellent way to include graphics on every printed page is to place them into the header and footer of your worksheet.

Include a Graphic in a Header or Footer

① Click the Insert tab.

② Click Header & Footer.

③ Click in the section of the header or footer where you want your graphic to appear.

④ Click the Picture button.

⑤ Navigate to the folder that contains the picture you want to insert.

⑥ Double-click the image.

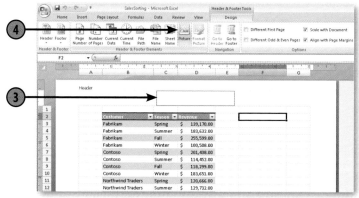

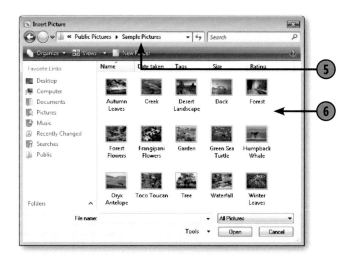

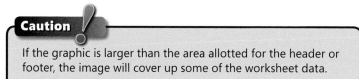

Caution

If the graphic is larger than the area allotted for the header or footer, the image will cover up some of the worksheet data.

Format a Graphic in a Header or Footer

① Click the Insert tab.

② Click Header & Footer.

③ Select the text & [Picture].

④ Click the Format Picture button.

⑤ Click the Size and Picture tabs and specify the options you want.

⑥ Click OK.

Caution

When using Format Picture, you cannot use the Undo button to reverse your actions after they've been completed.

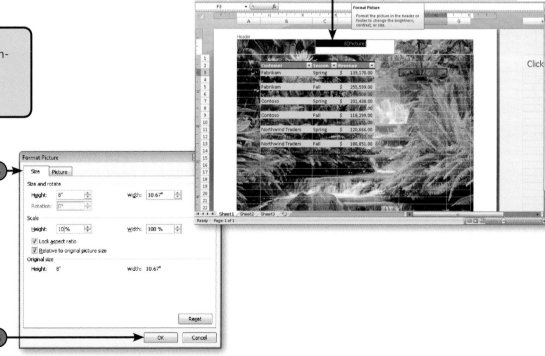

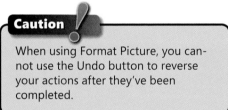

Setting and Viewing Page Breaks

Excel determines where one printed page ends and the next begins based on your page size, margins, and orientation; however, the page breaks Excel sets might not work for a particular worksheet. You might want to have a chart or table placed on its own sheet, or you might want to force two separate tables onto one printed page. You can display all existing page breaks by opening your worksheet in Page Break Preview

mode, which displays the page breaks as blue lines. If the blue lines are dashed, they represent an automatic page break; if the blue lines are solid, they represent a manually set page break. While in Page Break Preview, you can change the location of any existing page breaks to ensure your worksheets print exactly the way you want.

View Current Page Breaks

① Click the View tab.

② Click Page Break Preview.

Set Manual Page Breaks

① Click the cell the below and to the right of where you want to insert a page break.

② Click the Page Layout tab.

③ Click Breaks.

④ Click Insert Page Break.

⑤ On the status bar, click the Normal button to exit Page Break Preview.

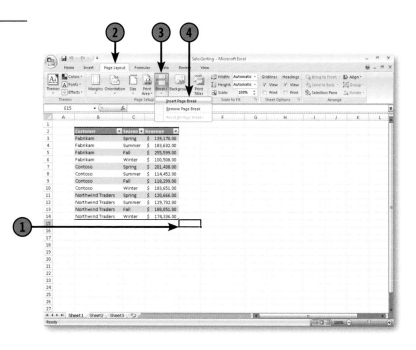

Change Manual Page Breaks

① Click the View tab.

② Click Page Break Preview.

③ Hover the mouse pointer over one of the blue lines until the mouse pointer becomes a two-headed arrow. Drag the line until the page break is where you want.

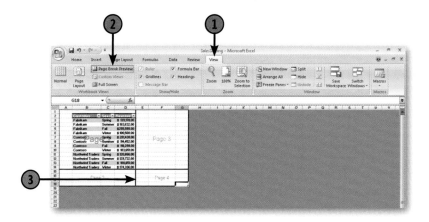

10

Customizing Excel to the Way You Work

Microsoft Excel gives you lots of ways to work with your data, with literally hundreds of commands at your disposal. You can access the vast majority of these commands by using the ribbon, but if you find that it takes several mouse clicks to reveal a command you use all the time, you can add the command you want to the Quick Access Toolbar so that you can activate it with a single click.

Another way to make your life easier is to create templates. A template is a workbook you use as a pattern for other workbooks. When you open a template, which is a separate Excel file type, you have the outline you need to create frequently used workbooks quickly.

You also have a great deal of control over how Excel handles the data you enter into your worksheets. Excel tries to be helpful by identifying formulas it thinks are mistakes, probably because the formula isn't consistent with other formulas near it or because it leaves out cells in a range. Sometimes those mistakes are exactly what you intended. The same is true for potential misspellings. Excel identifies and corrects the most common misspellings, but if a word Excel thinks is misspelled is actually correct, you can prevent Excel from making that change without turning off the corrective behavior entirely.

Opening Ready-to-Use Workbook Templates

When you have decided on the type of data you want to store in a workbook and what that workbook should look like, you probably will want to create similar workbooks without adding all the formatting and formulas again. For example, you might have settled on a design for your monthly sales tracking workbook. When you have settled on a design for your workbooks, you can save one of the workbooks as a pattern, or template, for similar workbooks you create in the future.

Create a Workbook from a Template

1 Click the Microsoft Office button.

2 Click New.

3 Click Installed Templates.

4 Double-click the template you want to use to create your workbook.

(continued on the next page)

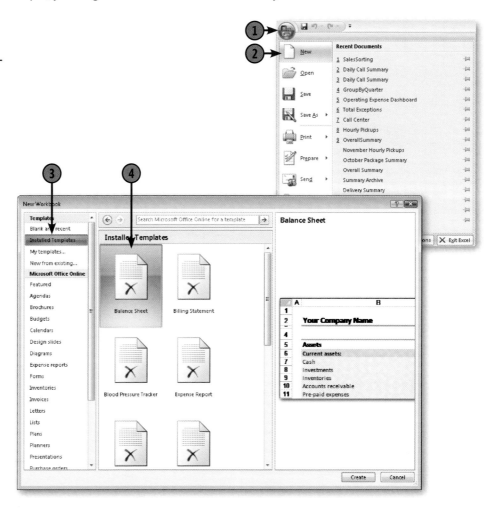

Create a Workbook from a
Template *(continued)*

⑤ Click the Microsoft Office button.

⑥ Click Save As.

⑦ Type a name for the file.

⑧ Click the Save As Type down arrow.

⑨ Click Excel Workbook.

⑩ Click Save.

Tip

If you have an active Internet connection, you can click one of the categories under Microsoft Office Online to display the templates available in the categories listed.

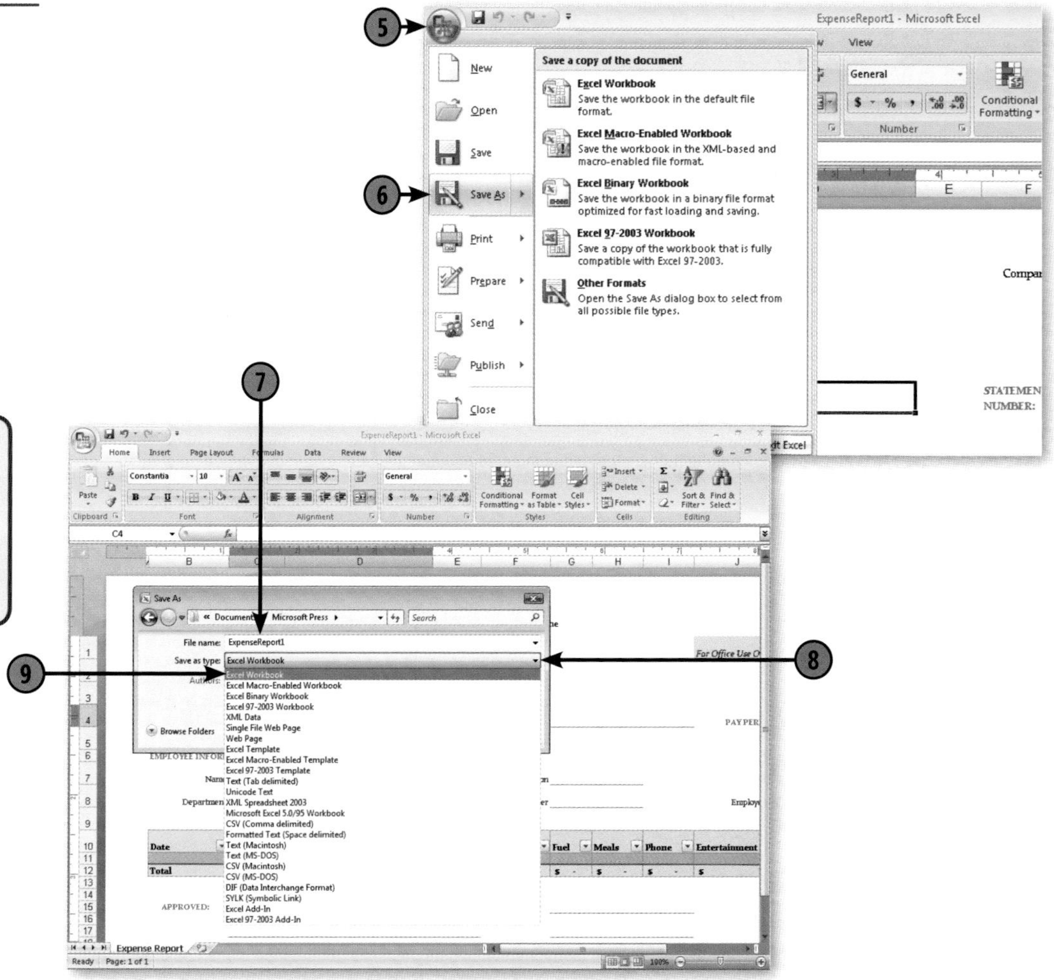

Modify a Template

① Click the Microsoft Office button.

② Click Open.

③ Click the template you want to modify.

④ Click Open.

⑤ Make the changes you want.

⑥ Click the Save button.

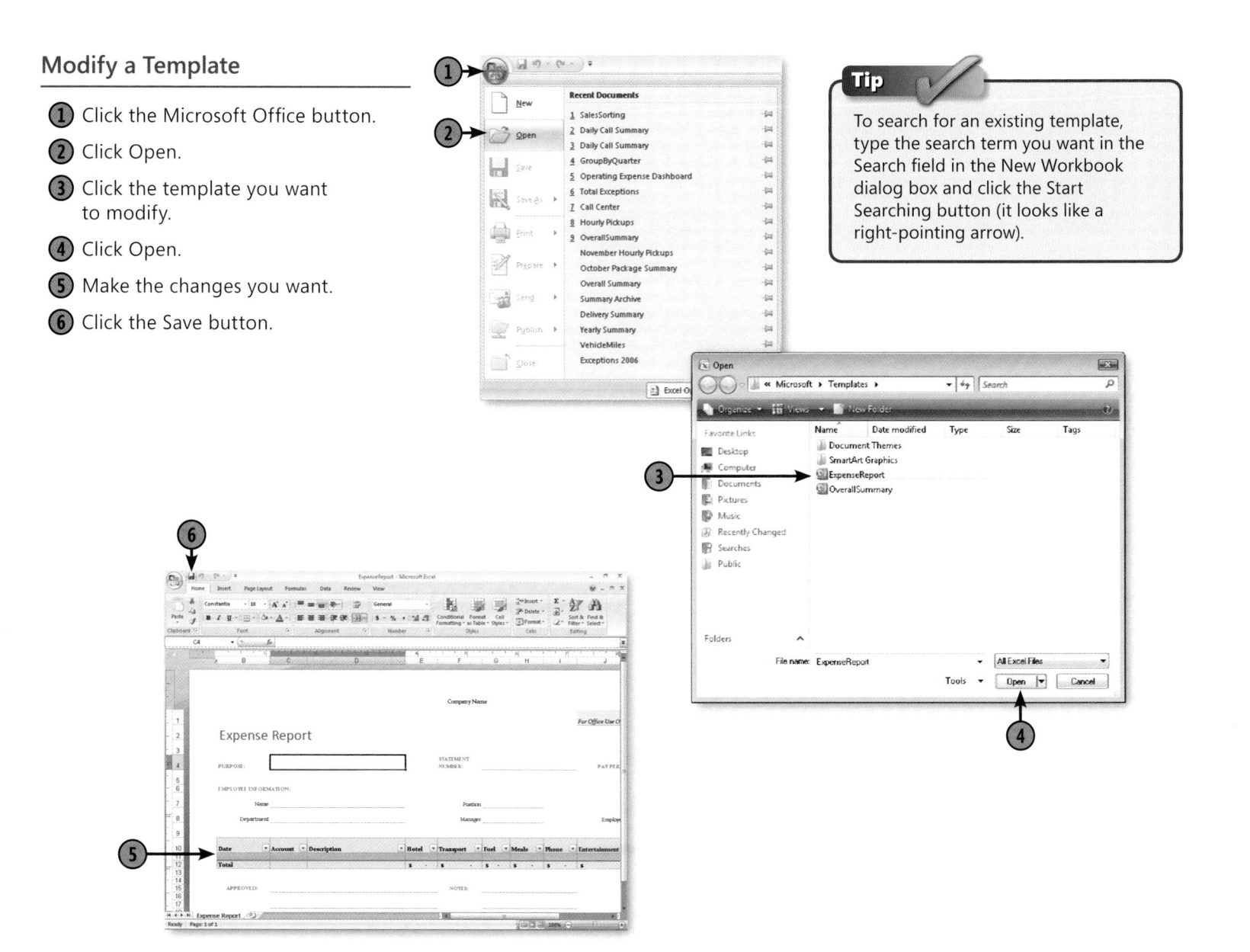

Tip

To search for an existing template, type the search term you want in the Search field in the New Workbook dialog box and click the Start Searching button (it looks like a right-pointing arrow).

Saving a Workbook as a Template

If you use the same workbook frequently, such as for entering the time you spent on projects during a week or tracking travel expenses, you will find that using a template saves you and your colleagues a lot of work. Saving a workbook is a straightforward process; all you need to do is create a workbook that contains the number of worksheets, formulas, and formatting you want and then save the workbook in the appropriate format.

Save a Workbook as a Template

1. Click the Microsoft Office button.

2. Click Save As.

3. Click the Save As Type down arrow.

4. Click Excel Template.

5. Type the name you want for the template.

6. Click Save.

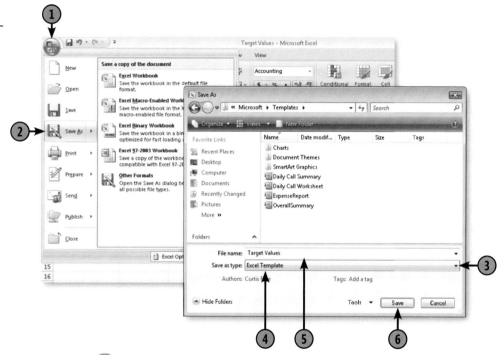

Caution

Be sure you don't change the directory where Excel offers to save your template. If you do change it, your template won't show up in the list of available templates. You could still open it by navigating to the folder in which you saved it, of course.

 Tip

You should remove any existing data from a workbook you save as a template, both to avoid data entry errors and to remove any confusion as to whether the workbook is a template. The one exception to this rule is when your template contains formulas that would result in an error if you delete all data from the worksheet. In that case, you should enter some obviously incorrect data that future users know to replace.

Adding Commands to the Quick Access Toolbar

The vast majority of commands you'll use in Excel 2007 appear on the ribbon, but some of the commands require you to move through one or two levels of the user interface (for example, click the correct ribbon tab and then click a button to open a dialog box). If there's a specific command you use all the time, you can make that command easier to find by adding it to the Quick Access Toolbar. If you later find that you don't use the command as much as you used to, you can always remove the command and make room for the commands you do use.

Add a Command to the Quick Access Toolbar

① Click the Microsoft Office button.

② Click Excel Options.

③ Click Customize.

④ Click the Choose Commands From down arrow.

⑤ Click the category from which you want to choose the command.

⑥ Click the command you want to add.

⑦ Click Add.

⑧ Click OK.

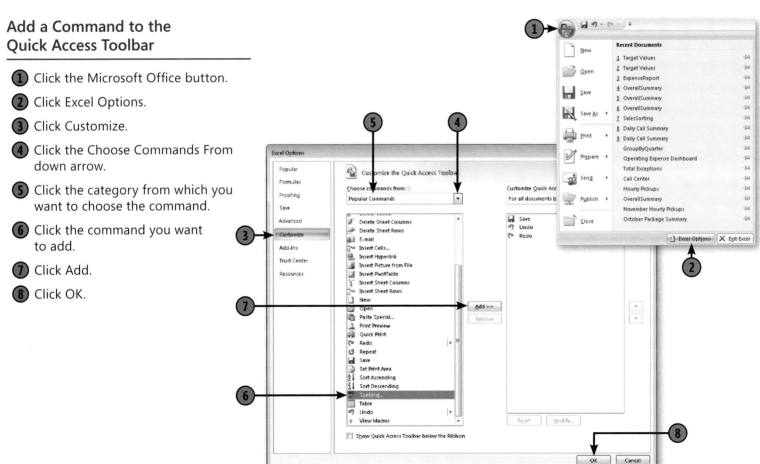

Remove a Command from the Quick Access Toolbar

(1) Click the Microsoft Office button.

(2) Click Excel Options.

(3) Click Customize.

(4) Click the command you want to remove.

(5) Click Remove.

(6) Click OK.

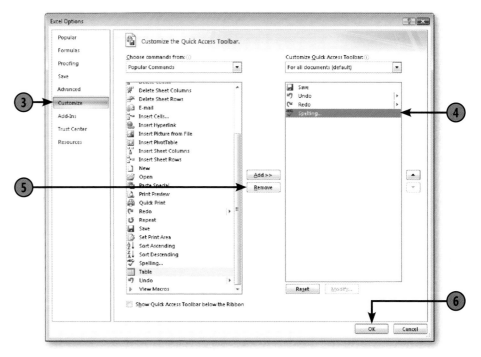

Move the Quick Access Toolbar

1 Click the Microsoft Office button.

2 Click Excel Options.

3 Click Customize.

4 Select the Show Quick Access Toolbar below the Ribbon check box.

5 Click OK.

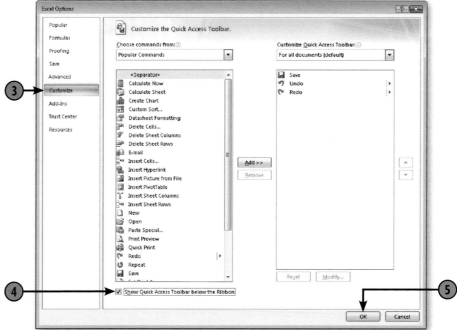

Controlling which Error Messages Appear

We all make mistakes, but some of those mistakes are easier to recover from than others. If you create a formula that tries to have Excel divide a value by zero or use a value from a cell that's currently blank, Excel will display an error flag indicating that it thinks you've made a mistake. If the error is that no value is in a cell you refer to in a formula, you can fix the problem by putting a value in that cell.

At times, though, Excel will identify a formula as an error when, in fact, it's exactly what you intended. For example, if

you create a worksheet that contains five columns of data, and you find the sum of each of those columns, Excel identifies the pattern inherent in those formulas. If you put a different type of formula (such as a formula that finds the maximum value in all five rows) in the cell next to those five consistent formulas, Excel will display an error indicating that the formula is inconsistent. Fortunately, you can choose to turn several types of error indicators on or off, saving you and your colleagues from worrying about errors that don't exist.

Choose which Error Messages Appear

① Click the Microsoft Office button.

② Click Excel Options.

③ Click Formulas.

④ Clear the check boxes next to the errors you want Excel to ignore.

⑤ Click OK.

Tip

The most common errors you'll want to ignore are formulas inconsistent with other formulas in the region and formulas that omit cells in a region.

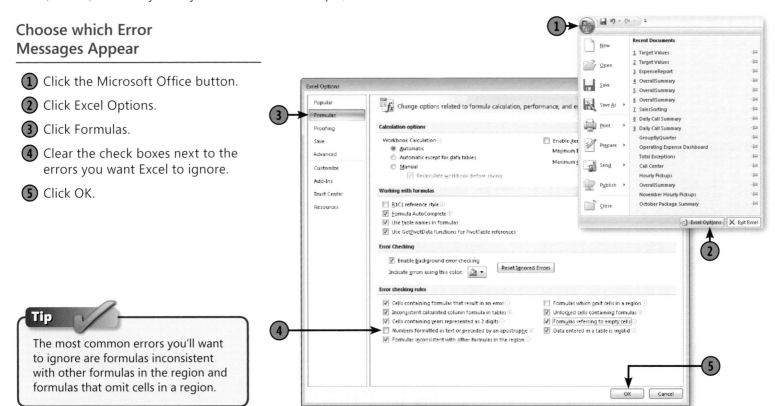

Reset Ignored Errors

① Click the Microsoft Office button.

② Click Excel Options.

③ Click Formulas.

④ Click Reset Ignored Errors.

⑤ Click OK.

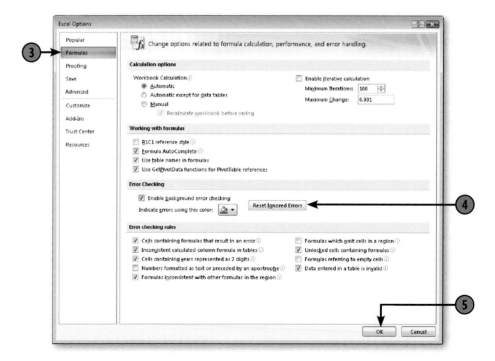

Select the Color in which Excel Displays Errors

① Click the Microsoft Office button.

② Click Excel Options.

③ Click Formulas.

④ Click Indicate Errors Using this Color.

⑤ Click the desired color.

⑥ Click OK.

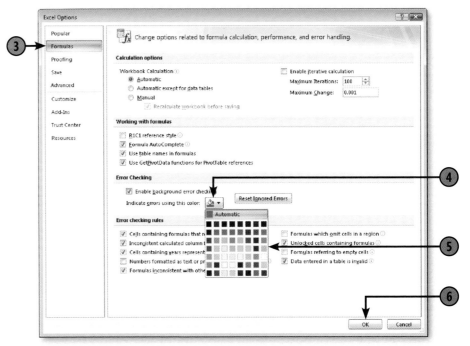

Defining AutoCorrect and AutoFormat Entries

You're bound to make typing mistakes when you spend a lot of time at the keyboard. In fact, slowing down doesn't help; the more slowly you go, the more likely you are to hit the wrong keys.

Over the years, many Excel users have allowed the programming team to monitor their typing, which means that the Excel team has been able to identify the most common mistakes resulting from popular misspellings, letter transpositions, and errors that are the result of not pressing the spacebar fast enough to put a space between words. If one of the words Excel identifies as an error is actually correct (for example, you work with a client corporation named Idae, a popular misspelling of the word idea), you can delete that entry from the AutoCorrect list.

Create an AutoCorrect Entry

1. Click the Microsoft Office button.

2. Click Excel Options.

3. Click Proofing.

4. Click AutoCorrect Options.

5. Type the text to be replaced.

6. Type the text to replace the previous entry.

7. Click Add.

8. Click OK to close the AutoCorrect dialog box

9. Click OK to close the Excel Options dialog box.

(continued on the next page)

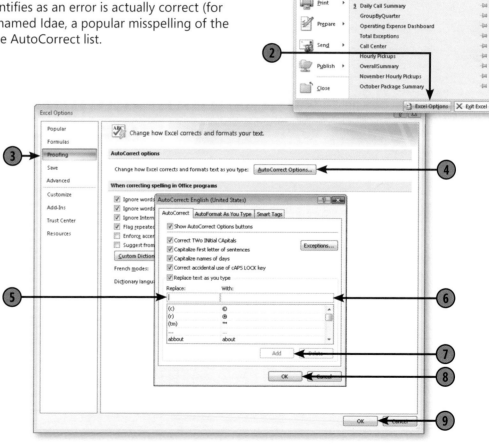

Create an AutoCorrect Entry *(continued)*

Tip

To undo an AutoCorrect correction, press Ctrl-Z.

Tip

Many users type the same text frequently, such as "Payment is due within 30 days. If payment is made within 10 days, you may deduct 2% from the total amount due." If you often typed that text, you could create an AutoCorrect entry that replaced the phrase Net30/2 with the text describing the payment terms already listed.

Delete an AutoCorrect Entry

1. Click the Microsoft Office button.
2. Click Excel Options.
3. Click Proofing.
4. Click AutoCorrect Options.
5. Click the entry to be removed.
6. Click Delete.
7. Click OK to close the AutoCorrect dialog box.
8. Click OK to close the Excel Options dialog box.

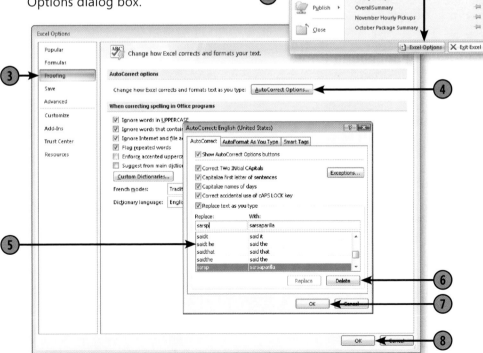

Control AutoFormat Rules

1. Click the Microsoft Office button.

2. Click Excel Options.

3. Click Proofing.

4. Click AutoCorrect Options.

5. Click the AutoFormat As You Type tab.

6. Clear the check boxes next to the rules you want to turn off or select the check boxes next to the rules you want to turn on.

7. Click OK to close the AutoCorrect dialog box.

8. Click OK to close the Excel Options dialog box.

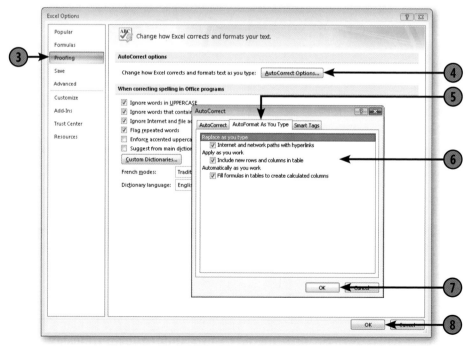

Controlling Worksheet Gridline Appearance

Excel 2007 enables you to decide whether to display a work-sheet's gridlines, which mark row, column, and cell boundaries. For worksheets that contain a lot of data, it's often a good idea to leave the gridlines on to help you distinguish between cells. For worksheets that contain charts and graphics, you should consider turning the gridlines off so they don't compete with the images. If you find that the default gridline color doesn't fit in with the rest of your design scheme, you can change that color as well.

Display or Hide
Worksheet Gridlines

① Click the View tab.

② Follow either of these steps:

- Clear the Gridlines check box to hide the worksheet's gridlines.

- Check the Gridlines check box to display the worksheet's gridlines.

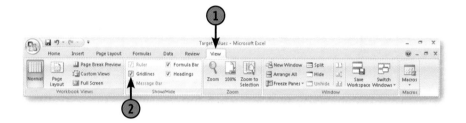

Change Gridline Color

① Click the Microsoft Office button.

② Click Excel Options.

③ Click Advanced.

④ In the Display options for this worksheet section, click Gridline color.

⑤ Click the desired color.

⑥ Click OK.

Tip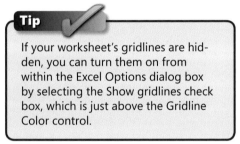

If your worksheet's gridlines are hidden, you can turn them on from within the Excel Options dialog box by selecting the Show gridlines check box, which is just above the Gridline Color control.

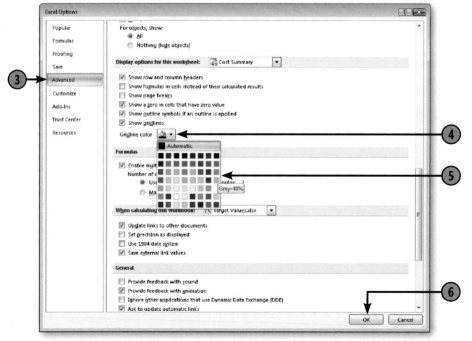

11

Sorting and Filtering Worksheet Data

After you've added data to your worksheets, you may want to change the order in which the worksheet rows are displayed. For example, if you had a worksheet listing orders for a week, you might want to list the orders for each customer, or perhaps reorder the rows in your worksheet so the most expensive orders were at the top of the list and the least expensive at the bottom. You could also hide any rows that didn't meet your criteria, which would be particularly useful if you work with a large data set.

Just as you can change or limit how your worksheet data is displayed, you can control what data is entered into your worksheets. By setting validation rules for groups of cells, you can check each value and, if the value you or your colleague enters falls outside the accepted range, you can display an error message informing you or your colleague what went wrong and what sort of value should be entered.

Sorting Worksheet Data

You can sort a group of rows in a worksheet in a number of ways, but the first step is identifying the column that will provide the values by which the rows should be sorted. When you've selected the column by which you want to sort the worksheet, you can choose whether to display the sorted values in ascending or descending order. For example, if you have a list of products your company sells with each product's sales in the same row, you could sort the worksheet by the contents of the sales column in descending order to discover which products generated the most revenue for your company. You could also sort the worksheet rows in ascending order to put the lowest-revenue products at the top of the list. If you want to sort by the contents of more than one column, you can create a multi-column sort. One handy use for a multi-column sort would be to sort your products by category and then by total sales.

Sort Data in Ascending or Descending Order

① Click any cell in the column by which you want to sort your data.

② Click the Data tab.

③ Follow either of these steps:

■ Click the Sort Ascending button in the Sort & Filter group on the ribbon.

■ Click the Sort Descending button in the Sort & Filter group on the ribbon.

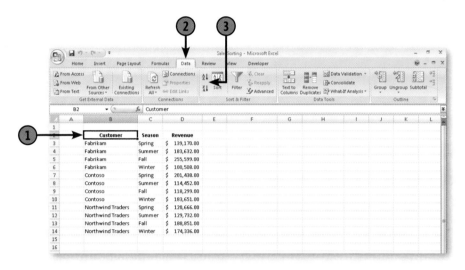

Tip

The names of the sorting buttons in the Data tab's Sort & Filter group change to reflect the type of data in the column to be sorted. If the column contains numbers, the buttons are named "Sort Smallest to Largest" and "Sort Largest to Smallest;" for text, the buttons are named "Sort A to Z" and "Sort Z to A;" for dates, they are named "Sort Oldest to Newest" and "Sort Newest to Oldest."

Create a Multi-Column Sort

① Select a cell in the data list or table you want to sort.

② Click the Data tab.

③ Click Sort.

④ Click the Sort By down arrow and then click the first column by which you want to sort.

⑤ Click the Sort On down arrow and then click the criteria by which you want to sort.

⑥ Click the Order down arrow.

⑦ Select the A to Z item or the Z to A item to indicate the order into which the column's values should be sorted.

⑧ Click Add Level.

⑨ If necessary, repeat steps 4–8 to set the columns and order for additional sorting rules.

⑩ Click OK.

Tip

In previous versions of Excel, you could sort a worksheet's contents by the values in up to only three columns. In Excel 2007, you can sort by the values in as many as 64 columns.

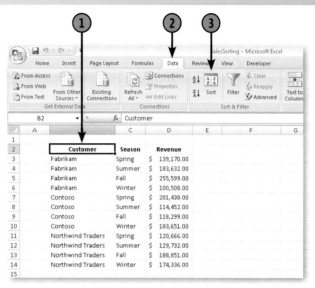

Caution

If you don't have a column with a unique value in each cell, such as a product number or customer identification number, you might not be able to put your worksheet back into its original order.

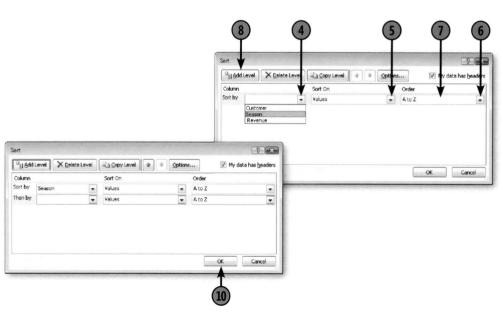

Creating a Custom Sort List

When you sort column data, Excel sorts numbers according to their values and words in alphabetical order, but that pattern doesn't work for some sets of values. For example, sorting the months of the year in alphabetical order would put February in front of January. To avoid those errors, Excel comes with four custom lists: days of the week, abbreviations for days of the week, months, and abbreviated month names. You can have Excel sort based on those lists or, if you want to create a custom list of your own, you can do so. Because the day and abbreviated day name lists begin with Sunday, you could create a new list beginning with Monday to reflect your business schedule.

Define a Custom List of Values

1. Click the Microsoft Office button.
2. Click Excel Options.
3. Click Popular.
4. Click Edit Custom Lists.
5. Click New List.
6. Type the custom list you want. Separate each entry by pressing Enter.
7. Click Add.
8. Click OK twice to close the Custom Lists dialog box and the Excel Options dialog box.

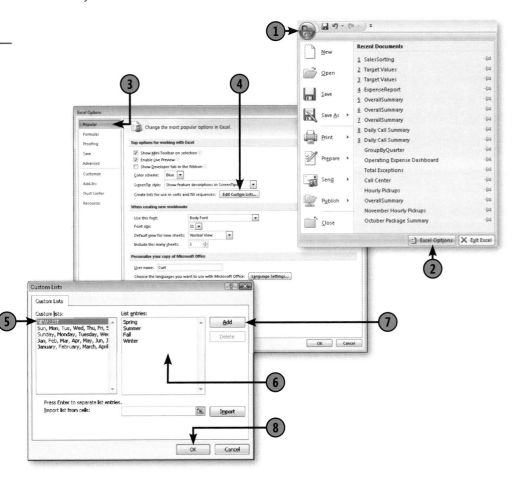

Sort by a Custom List

① Click any cell in the list you want to sort.

② Click the Data tab.

③ Click Sort.

④ Click the Sort By down arrow and then click the column you want to sort by.

⑤ Click the Sort On down arrow and then click the criteria you want to sort by.

⑥ Click the Order down arrow and then click Custom List.

⑦ Click a custom list.

⑧ Click OK to close the Custom Lists dialog box.

⑨ Click OK to sort the data list.

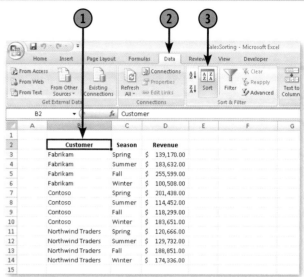

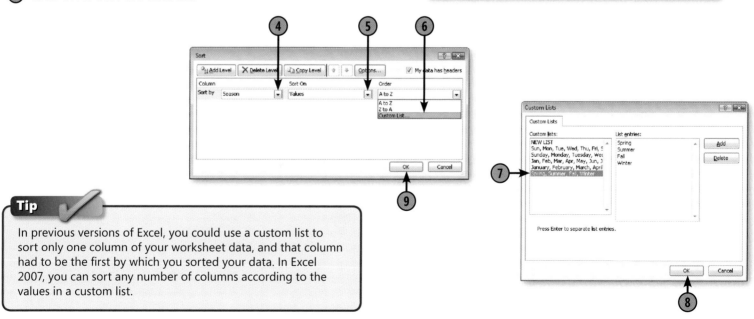

Tip ✓

In previous versions of Excel, you could use a custom list to sort only one column of your worksheet data, and that column had to be the first by which you sorted your data. In Excel 2007, you can sort any number of columns according to the values in a custom list.

Filtering Data Quickly with AutoFilter

An important aspect of working with large amounts of data is the ability to zero in on the most important data in a worksheet, whether that data represents the best 10 days of sales in a month or slow-selling product lines you may need to re-evaluate. In Microsoft Excel, you have a number of powerful, flexible techniques you can use to limit the data displayed in your worksheet. One of those techniques is to filter the contents of a workbook. Unlike sorting, which arranges worksheet rows according to rules you set, filtering a worksheet hides rows that don't meet the rules you define.

Create an AutoFilter

1 Click any cell in the range you want to filter.

2 Click the Data tab.

3 Click Filter.

4 Click the filter arrow for the column by which you want to filter your worksheet.

5 Select the check boxes next to the values by which you want to filter the list.

6 Click OK.

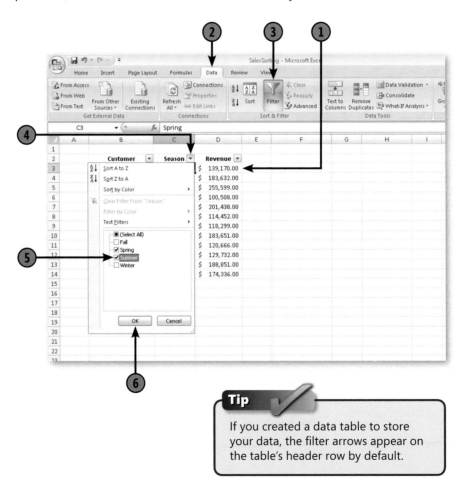

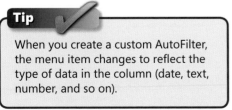

Tip

When you create a custom AutoFilter, the menu item changes to reflect the type of data in the column (date, text, number, and so on).

Tip

If you created a data table to store your data, the filter arrows appear on the table's header row by default.

Display All Rows in a Filtered List

1. Click the filter arrow of the filtered column.

2. Click the Select All check box.

3. Click OK.

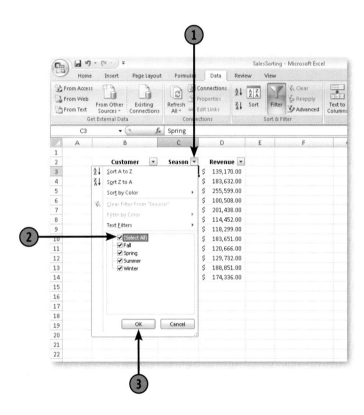

Create a Custom AutoFilter

① Click any cell in the list you want to filter.

② Click the Data tab.

③ If necessary, click Filter to display the filter arrows.

④ Click the filter arrow of the column for which you want to create a custom filter.

⑤ Point to Text Filters.

⑥ Click Custom Filter.

⑦ Click the Comparison Operator down arrow.

⑧ Click the comparison you want to use.

⑨ Type the value by which you want to compare the values in the selected column.

⑩ Click OK.

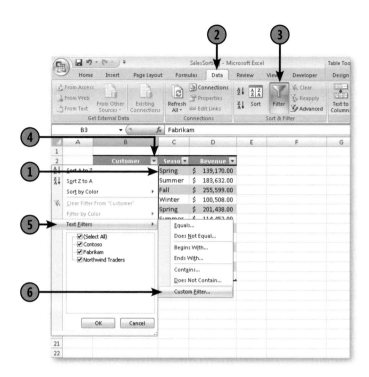

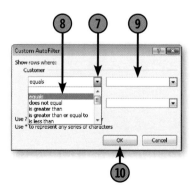

Tip

When a column is filtered, the filter arrow that appears to the right of the filtered list header is replaced by a filter icon.

Creating an Advanced Filter

When you create a filter using AutoFilter, you can create complex rules to filter the contents of the worksheet. The limitation is that the rules used to filter the worksheet aren't readily discernable. If you want the rules used to filter a column's values to be displayed in the body of the worksheet, you can write each rule in a cell and identify those cells so Excel knows how to filter the worksheet. If you ever want to change the rules used to filter your data, all you need to do is change a rule and reapply the filter.

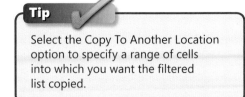

Tip Select the Copy To Another Location option to specify a range of cells into which you want the filtered list copied.

Build an Advanced Filter

(1) Copy the column titles of the list you want to filter.

(2) Paste the titles in another spot on your workbook.

(3) Under their respective titles, type the criteria you want met.

(4) Select a cell in the list you want filtered.

(5) Click the Data tab.

(6) In the Sort & Filter group on the ribbon, click Advanced.

(7) Click the List Range box.

(8) Select the entire list you want to filter, including the column headers.

(9) Click the Criteria Range box.

(10) Select the cells on which you want to base the filter, including the column headers.

(11) Click OK.

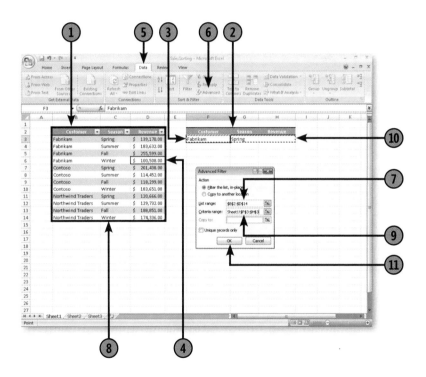

Remove an Advanced Filter

① Select the cells from which you want to remove a filter.

② Click the Data tab.

③ In the Sort & Filter group on the ribbon, click Clear.

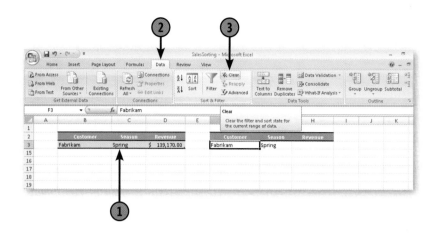

Validating Data for Correctness during Entry

Just as you can limit the data displayed by your worksheets, you can limit the data entered into them as well. Setting validation rules for data entered into cells lets you catch many of the most common data-entry errors, such as entering values that are too small or too large or attempting to enter a word in a cell that requires a number. When you create a validation rule, you can also create a message to inform you and your colleagues what sort of data is expected for the cell.

Validate for Specific Requirements

① Select the cells you want to validate.

② On the Data tab, click the Data Validation button's down arrow.

③ Click Data Validation.

(continued on the next page)

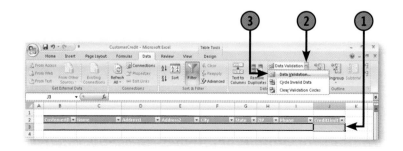

Validate for Specific
Requirements *(continued)*

④ Click the Allow down arrow.

⑤ Click the type of data you want to allow.

⑥ Click the Data down arrow and click the condition for which you want to validate.

⑦ Type the appropriate values in the boxes.

⑧ Click the Input Message tab.

⑨ Select the Show Input Message When Cell Is Selected check box.

⑩ Type the message you want to appear when the cell is clicked.

⑪ Click the Error Alert tab.

⑫ Select the Show Error Alert After Invalid Data is Entered check box.

⑬ Click the Style down arrow.

⑭ Click the icon you want to appear next to your message.

⑮ Type a title for the error message box.

⑯ Type the error message you want.

⑰ Click OK.

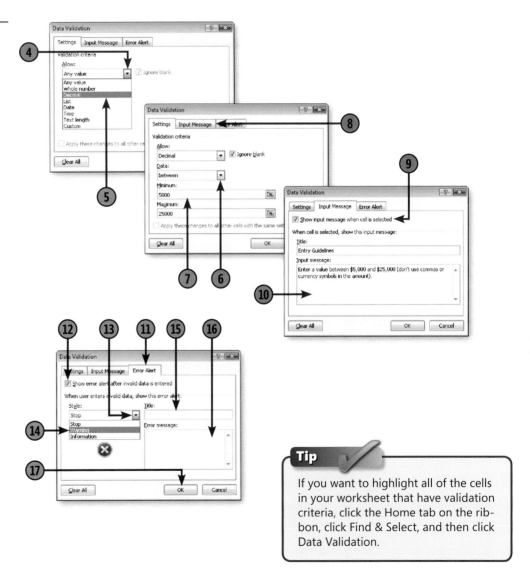

Tip ✓

If you want to highlight all of the cells in your worksheet that have validation criteria, click the Home tab on the ribbon, click Find & Select, and then click Data Validation.

Validate Data According to a List in a Worksheet Range

(1) Select the cells that you want to validate.

(2) On the Data tab, click the Data Validation button's down arrow.

(3) Click Data Validation.

(4) Click the Settings tab.

(5) Click the Allow down arrow.

(6) Click List.

(7) Click the Source box.

(8) Select the cells that contain the values you want in your list.

(9) Click OK.

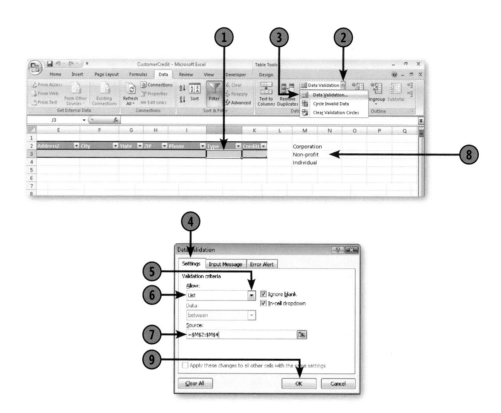

Tip

In the Settings tab of the Data Validation dialog box, you can clear the In-Cell drop-down button so that a drop-down arrow does not appear next to the cell with the available options.

Tip

To validate the entire workbook, hold down the Ctrl key and press the **A** key to select the entire workbook. Then apply the data validation criteria.

Tip

If you don't want to display the list items in your workbook, you can type them out in the dialog box. Be sure to separate the items with commas (,).

Getting More out of Advanced Filters

You can use Advanced Filters to limit the rows that appear in your worksheet, but their utility doesn't stop there. In addition to setting multiple criteria to filter your worksheet, you can use Advanced Filters to copy the filter's results to another group of cells on any Microsoft Excel worksheet. Copying the results of an Advanced Filter saves you time by identifying where you want the results of your filter to be pasted. Rather than applying the filter and manually copying the results to the new location, you can identify the destination when you create the filter.

Copy Filtered Rows to a New Location

1. Copy the column titles of the list you want to filter.

2. Paste the titles in another spot on your workbook.

3. Under their respective titles, type the criteria you want met.

4. Select a cell in the list you want filtered.

5. Click the Data tab.

6. In the Sort & Filter group on the ribbon, click Advanced.

7. Select the Copy To Another Location option.

8. Click the List Range box.

9. Select the entire list you want to filter, including the column headers.

10. Click the Criteria Range box.

11. Select the cells with the filtering criteria.

12. Click in the Copy To box.

13. Select the cell at the top left corner of where you want the filtered rows to be placed.

14. Click OK.

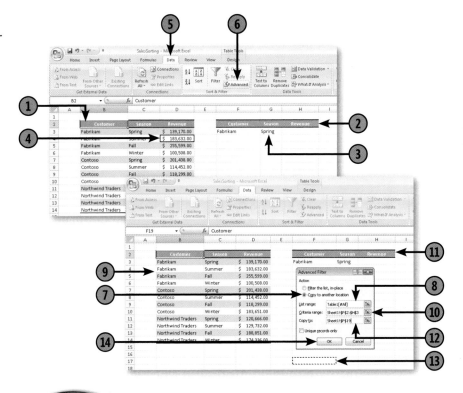

See Also

For more information on assigning criteria for an Advanced Filter, see "Creating an Advanced Filter" on page 187.

Finding Unique Values in a Data List

When you have Excel locate unique values in a worksheet, you create an Advanced Filter that finds every value that occurs within a single column you identify. For example, if you had a list of all sales on a given day, you could identify which sales representatives made at least one sale. One important limitation of finding unique values, however, is that identification works on only worksheets in which the data is limited to the

columns in which you want to find unique values. For example, if you had a two-column worksheet listing the OrderID of an order and the sales representative who took the order, every row would have a unique combination of OrderID (which is different for every order) and sales representative. To find sales representatives who had made a sale on that day, you would need to delete the OrderID column.

Find Unique Rows in a Data Table

1. Select the cells in which you want to find unique values.

2. Click the Data tab.

3. Click Advanced.

4. Select the Unique Records Only check box.

5. Click OK.

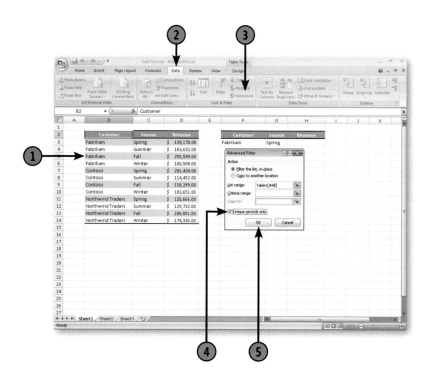

Finding Duplicate Values in a Data List

When you maintain organizational records in an Excel data list, you must be careful not to enter an order, customer, or supplier into your list more than once. As an example, suppose that you own a business and accidentally created two customer information records for the same customer. If you generate a mass mailing, that customer would receive two copies of your mailer, costing you money. What's worse, if you and your employees don't realize the customer is in your list twice, and each entry has its own CustomerID value (like the customer number you see on catalogs mailed to your home or business), you could end up assigning some sales to one ID and some to the other. Should the customer call to ask about an order, your employees might not be able to find it because they're looking up the customer's information using the "wrong" CustomerID value.

Delete Duplicate Values from a Data List

① Click any cell in the data list.

② Click the Data tab.

③ Click Remove Duplicates.

④ Select and clear check boxes to indicate the columns you want Excel to consider when it searches for duplicate rows.

⑤ Click OK.

⑥ Click OK to clear the message box indicating how many rows were deleted and how many remain.

Caution

Excel doesn't ask whether you want to delete the rows; it just deletes them. Clicking the Undo button on the Quick Access Toolbar will restore the rows to the list, but if your list has fewer than a few hundred rows, you should consider using a combination of sorting and filtering to identify duplicate entries.

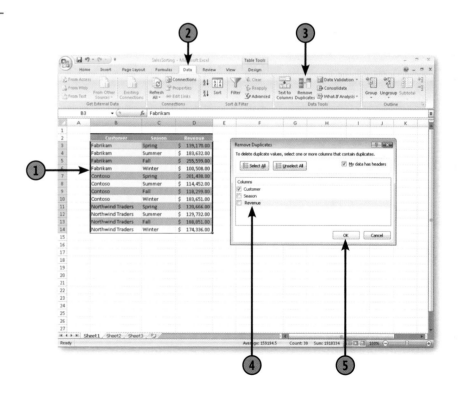

12

Summarizing Data Visually Using Charts

Excel gives you lots of ways to change how your numeric data is displayed. You can change the color or font of data you want to emphasize, make your labels bold to set them apart from the body of data in your worksheets, and add graphics to establish your corporate identity. You can use totals and subtotals to summarize your data, making it easier for you and your colleagues to compare values for entire categories of data.

The limitation of working with numbers, even in summary, is that it can be difficult to keep track of several numbers at a time. If you've worked for several years in a package delivery company, you might know that November and December are the busiest months of the year and that February and March show the lowest package volume. If you're presenting the results to colleagues or potential investors who are less familiar with your business, you can use charts and graphs to summarize your data visually. By summarizing your data using a chart, you make it much easier for your colleagues to see patterns and relationships.

Displaying Data Graphically

When you enter data into a Microsoft Excel worksheet, you create a record of important events, whether they are individual product sales, sales for an hour of a day, or the price of a product. What a list of values in cells can't communicate easily, however, are the overall trends in your data. The best way to communicate trends in large data collections is through charts and graphs, which summarize data visually.

As an example of how charts and graphs can help present your data more effectively, consider the following data table, which lists the travel expenses for a company's sales force.

Category	Expenses
Car	$ 29,560.00
Lodging	$ 100,053.00
Meals	$ 46,729.00
Misc	$ 28,207.00
Plane	$ 201,872.00

In a sense, the data does speak for itself. The total expenses for each category are listed so you and your colleagues can compare them. Each number must be comprehended, remembered, and compared to the other results individually. When you present the results in a chart or graph, as is done with the following column chart, you can compare the values more readily.

If you have trouble deciding which type of chart or graph you should create, you can experiment while you build a chart. The following chart gallery explains which types of data each chart type can be used to represent effectively, but feel free to experiment!

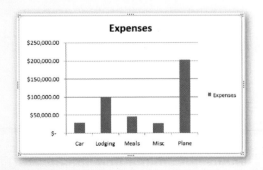

Standard Excel Chart Types and Uses

Chart Type	Use
Column	Compares data in vertical format.
Bar	Compares data in horizontal format.
Line	Compares data in a line format.
Pie	Compares the data in a percent format.
Scatter Plot	Compares pairs of values in a dot format.
Area	Compares the trend of values over time or categories.
Doughnut	Compares multiple series of data in a percent format.
Radar	Displays changes in values relative to a center point.
Surface	Displays trends in values across two dimensions.
Bubble	Compares sets of three values.
Stock	Displays a chart to compare stock prices and quotes.
Cylinder	Same as a column or bar chart, but a cylinder is used instead.
Cone	Same as a column or bar chart, but a cone is used instead.
Pyramid	Same as a column or bar chart, but a pyramid is used instead.

Creating a Chart Quickly

To present your Excel data graphically, select the cells you want to summarize, click the Insert tab, and then use the controls in the chart gallery to select the chart type that's best for your data and the message you want to get across. The cells with the data to be represented in the chart are part of one or more data series. A series is a collection of related data, such as all sales for a particular product or the sales for each day of a month. A bar chart could contain just one series; a line chart, which might display monthly sales for several years, could have many series.

Creating attractive charts is much easier in Excel 2007 than in previous versions of the program. Not only can you create the chart quickly by using the controls on the ribbon, you can use the same controls to choose your chart's overall layout and style. After you set your chart's general appearance, you can make any desired changes with no trouble at all.

Create a Chart

① Click a cell in the data list you want to summarize.

② Click the Insert tab.

③ Click the type of chart you want to create.

④ Click the desired chart subtype.

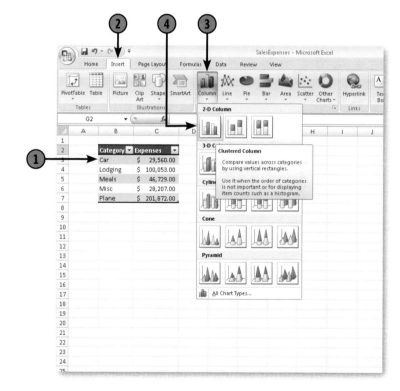

> **Tip**
>
> Pressing F11 creates a chart of the default type (a column chart, unless you've changed it), with the default layout and formatting, on a new workbook sheet.

Change a Chart's Layout

1. Click the chart you want to change.

2. Click the Design tab.

3. In the Chart Layouts group on the ribbon, click the desired layout.

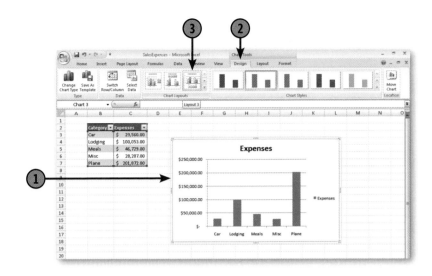

Change a Chart's Style

1. Click the chart you want to change.

2. Click the Design tab.

3. In the Chart Styles group on the ribbon, click the desired style.

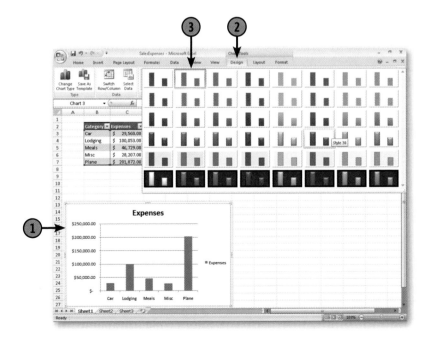

Changing a Chart's Appearance

After you've created a chart, you can change any part of its appearance, including the chart's type! If you display monthly sales data as a series of columns and decide that you would like to show the data as a line rising and falling as it moves from month to month, you can change the chart's type at will. You can also change the color, font, and other properties of any chart element. If you want your chart's title to be displayed in your company's official font, you can format the title easily.

Change a Chart's Type

1. Click the chart you want to change.
2. Click the Design tab.
3. Click Change Chart Type.
4. Click the type of chart you want.
5. Click the desired chart subtype and click OK.

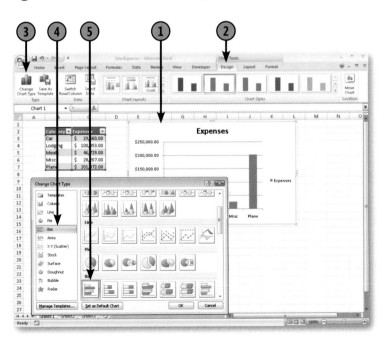

Change the Formatting of a Chart Element

1. Click the chart element you want to change.
2. Click the Format tab.
3. Use the controls in the Shape Styles group to format the chart element.

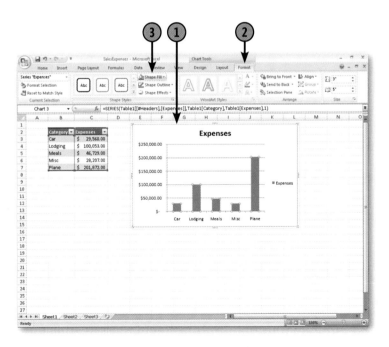

Formatting Chart Legends and Titles

An important part of creating an informative, easily read chart is to describe the contents of the chart. Some chart elements you can add to describe your Excel charts are legends, titles, data labels, and annotations. A legend is an index of categories in a chart and the color used to describe them. A sales chart comparing monthly sales for several years, for example, might display the first year in yellow, the second year in blue, and the third year in red. The legend identifies those relationships so you can read the chart accurately. Titles, data labels, and annotations describe specific parts of a chart or, in the case of annotations, give general information about the data the chart displays.

Show or Hide a Chart Legend

① Click the chart you want to format.

② Click the Layout tab.

③ Click Legend.

④ Click the desired legend display option.

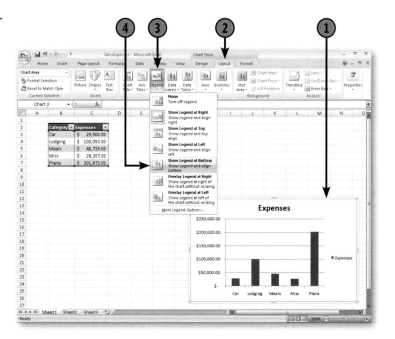

Add Titles

① Click the chart you want to format.

② Click the Layout tab.

③ Click Chart Title.

④ Click the desired title display option.

⑤ Click the title and then type the new title for the chart.

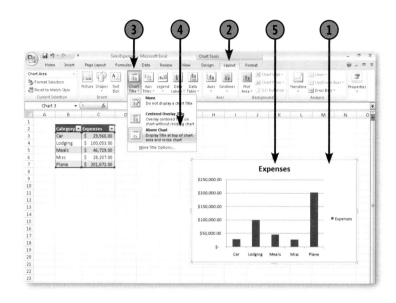

Add and Remove Data Labels

① Click the chart you want to format.

② Click the Layout tab.

③ Click Data Labels.

④ Click the desired data label option.

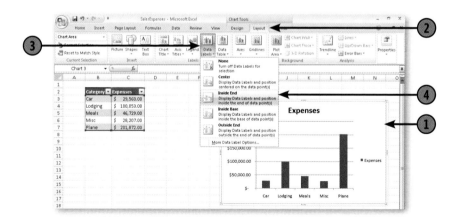

Changing the Body of a Chart

When you add labels, a legend, or annotations to a chart, you change the periphery of the chart, but you don't affect how the data is displayed. If you do want to change how the data is displayed in the body of the chart, such as by showing or hiding grid lines or changing the scale of the chart, you can

do so. Adding grid lines can help viewers make fine distinctions between values, even if they're viewing the chart from the other end of a conference table, while changing the scale of the chart lets you heighten or downplay the differences among the chart's values.

Show or Hide Chart Grid Lines

1 Click the chart you want to format.

2 Click the Layout tab.

3 Click Gridlines.

4 Click the set of gridlines you want to change.

5 Click the desired gridline display option.

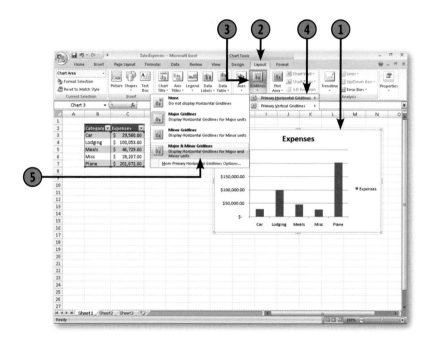

Change the Scale on the Value Axis

① Click the chart you want to format.

② Click the Layout tab.

③ Click Axes.

④ Click Primary Vertical Axis.

⑤ Click More Primary Vertical Axis Options.

⑥ Click Axis Options.

⑦ Click the Minimum row's Fixed option button and then type a value for the minimum value on the vertical axis.

⑧ Click the Maximum row's Fixed option button and then type a value for the maximum value on the vertical axis.

⑨ Click the Major Unit row's Fixed option button and then type a value for the major units to be displayed on the vertical axis.

⑩ Click the Minor Unit row's Fixed option button and then type a value for the minor units to be displayed on the vertical axis.

⑪ Click Close.

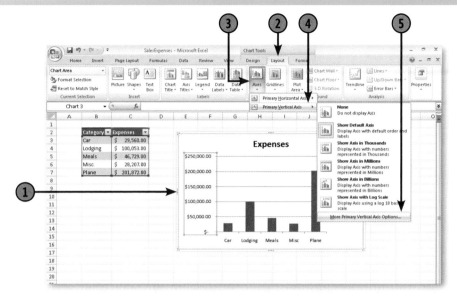

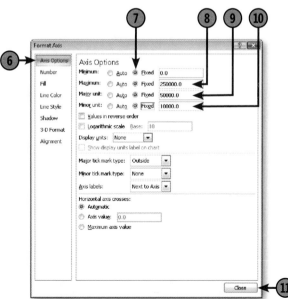

Change the Scale on the Category (X) Axis

① Click the chart you want to format.

② Click the Layout tab.

③ Click Axes.

④ Click Primary Horizontal Axis.

⑤ Click More Primary Horizontal Axis Options.

⑥ If necessary, click the Axis Options tab.

⑦ Enter how often you want the tick-marks to appear.

⑧ Select the Specify Interval Unit option button.

⑨ Enter how often you want the tick-mark labels to appear.

⑩ Select or clear the other options.

⑪ Click Close.

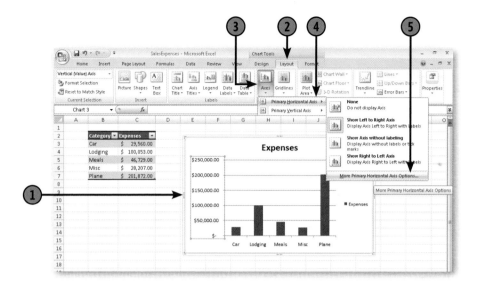

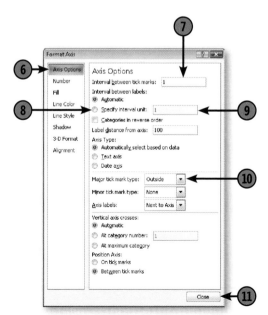

Customizing Chart Data

Whenever you create a chart for a business, there's always the possibility that the data displayed in the chart will change. Whether those changes reflect continuing sales, updated values that account for returns and inventory charges, or investment projections revised to match market conditions, you can update your chart by identifying a new data source. The data can be in any workbook on your computer or network—all you need to do is identify the cells with the data, and Excel will do the rest.

Change the Source Data for Your Chart

① Click the chart you want to change.

② Click the Design tab.

③ Click Select Data.

④ Click in the Chart Data Range field.

⑤ Select the cells you want to provide the new source data.

⑥ Click OK.

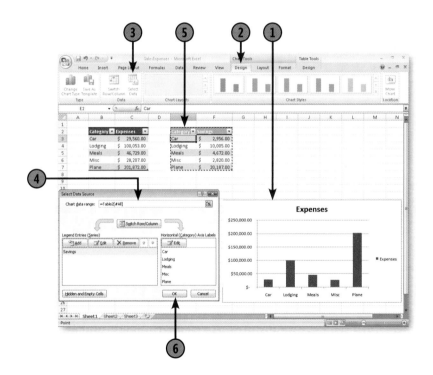

Add a New Series

1. Click the chart you want to change.

2. Click the Design tab.

3. Click Select Data.

4. Click Add.

5. Type the name you want to assign to the series.

6. Click in the Series Values field.

7. Select the cells you want to add.

8. Click OK to close the Edit Series dialog box.

9. Click OK to close the Select Data Source dialog box.

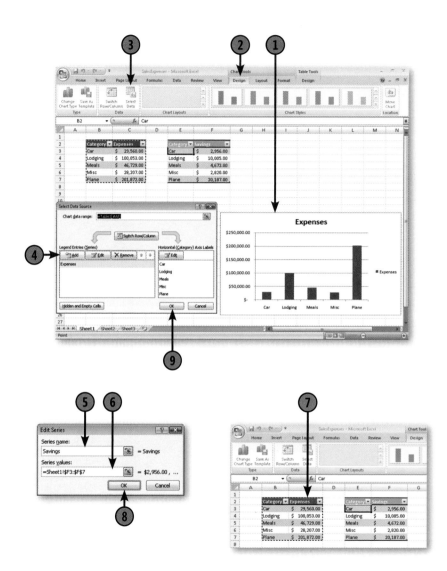

Tip

You can also type the address of the cell that contains the series name you want to use in the chart.

Add a New Series

1. Click the chart you want to change.

2. Click the Design tab.

3. Click Select Data.

4. Click Add.

5. Type the name you want to assign to the series.

6. Click in the Series Values field.

7. Select the cells you want to add.

8. Click OK to close the Edit Series dialog box.

9. Click OK to close the Select Data Source dialog box.

Tip

You can also type the address of the cell that contains the series name you want to use in the chart.

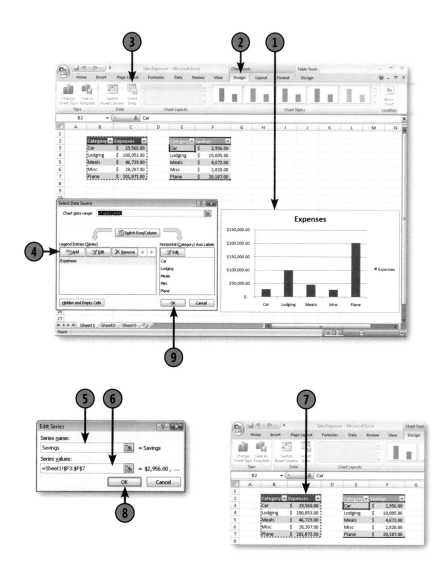

Customizing Chart Data

Whenever you create a chart for a business, there's always the possibility that the data displayed in the chart will change. Whether those changes reflect continuing sales, updated values that account for returns and inventory charges, or investment projections revised to match market conditions, you can update your chart by identifying a new data source. The data can be in any workbook on your computer or network—all you need to do is identify the cells with the data, and Excel will do the rest.

Change the Source Data for Your Chart

① Click the chart you want to change.

② Click the Design tab.

③ Click Select Data.

④ Click in the Chart Data Range field.

⑤ Select the cells you want to provide the new source data.

⑥ Click OK.

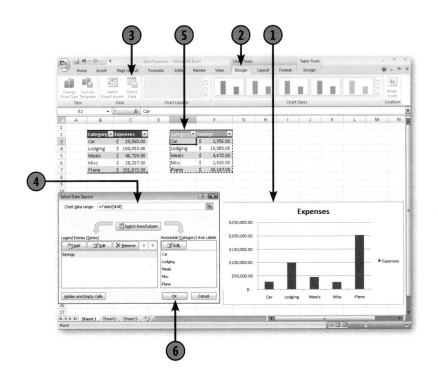

Delete a Series

1. Click the chart you want to change.

2. Click the Design tab.

3. Click Select Data.

4. Click the name of the series you want to delete.

5. Click Remove.

6. Click OK.

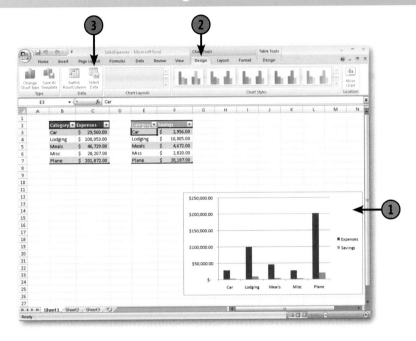

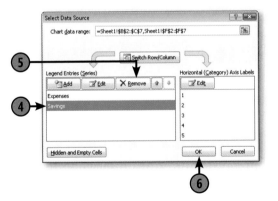

Working with Common Charts

One chart type you'll probably work with quite frequently is the pie chart, which displays the contribution of a series of values to the total of those values. Each section represents a category of data, such as a month in a year or a category of product. One way you can extend the capabilities of a basic pie chart and emphasize part of the data is to pull one section of the pie away from the rest of the chart. You can also change how you look at a three-dimensional chart, moving closer or farther away from the chart and changing your perspective.

Pull a Slice Out of a Pie Chart

1. Click the body of the pie chart you want to change.

2. Click the piece of data you want to separate.

3. Drag the piece away from the pie.

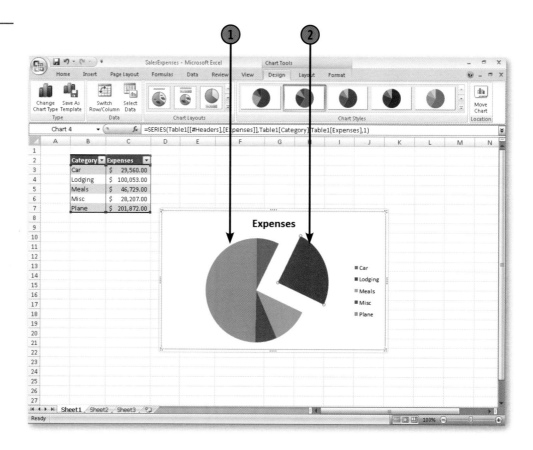

Create a 3-D Exploded Pie Chart

① Click a cell in the data list you want to summarize in the pie chart.

② Click the Insert tab.

③ Click Pie.

④ Click the second chart type under the 3-D Pie heading.

Tip

If you want to remove the explosion effect from a pie chart, drag the data of the pie chart toward the center of the pie.

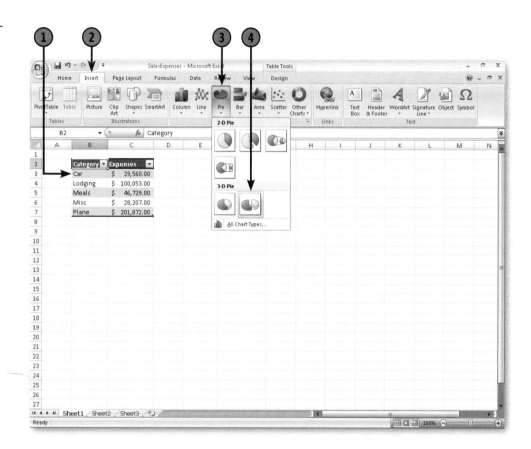

Change the Way You View 3-D Charts

① Click the chart element you want to format.

② Click the Format tab.

③ Click Shape Effects.

④ Click Shadow.

⑤ Click the desired shadow setting.

Caution

Not all 3-D options are available for all chart types.

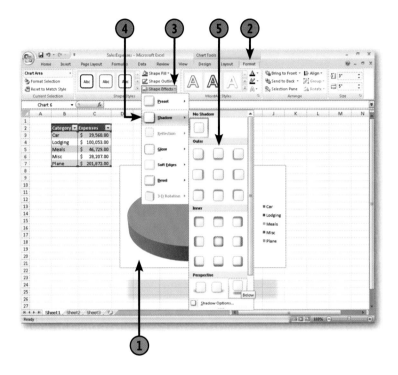

Working with Uncommon Charts

When you pick a type of chart or graph to present your data, you'll probably consider pie charts, line graphs, and bar charts. Those chart types are used most often because of their familiarity and their straightforward presentation of the relation- ships between elements of a data series. You can use other types of charts, however, when appropriate. One of those chart types is the stock chart, which you can use to present stock market data.

Create a Stock Chart

1. Select the stock data you want to chart. Be sure the data is formatted as shown in the figure.

2. Click the Insert tab.

3. Click Other Charts.

4. Click a Stock chart subtype.

Tip

Several stock chart subtypes are available, each of which requires a different set of data columns. When you hover the mouse pointer over a chart subtype, Excel displays information about the subtype and the data it requires.

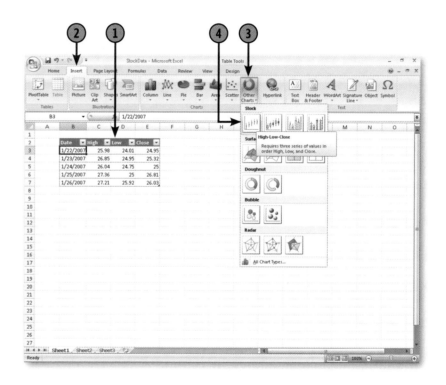

Adding a Trendline to a Chart

You can use the data in your Excel workbooks to analyze past performance, but you can also have Excel make its best guess as to future performance if current trends continue. For example, if you create a chart that represents your company's sales for the past five years, you can have Excel analyze the data and add a trendline to the chart to represent how much sales would increase if the current trend holds true for the next year.

Add a Trendline to a Data Series

1. Click the chart to which you want to add a trendline.

2. Click the data series to which you want to add a trendline.

3. Click the Layout tab.

4. Click Trendline.

5. Click Linear Forecast Trendline.

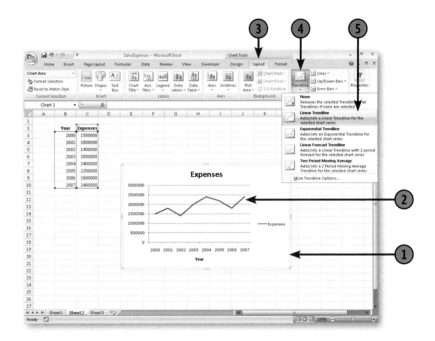

Tip

If you'd like more control over your trendline, such as by choosing a different mathematical procedure to extend the line (although the default Linear option works the vast majority of the time) or by choosing the number of units by which to extend the line, click Trendline and then click More Trendline Options to display the Format Trendline dialog box.

Caution

Unless you're working with certain types of scientific data and you know that your trendline requires a logarithmic, exponential, or other regression type, select the Linear Trendline option. If you don't, you won't get accurate results!

13

Enhancing Your Worksheets with Graphics

When you create a worksheet, your first consideration is to ensure that the data is stored in an understandable format and that all of the formulas produce the expected results. After you've taken care of the worksheet's structure, however, you should ensure that you and your colleagues can comprehend the data easily. One way you can help you and your colleagues understand the data in your worksheet is to add drawing objects, such as boxes, stars, and banners, to make your annotations and labels stand out.

Another way you can present business data in an Excel worksheet is to create a diagram. In Excel, diagrams encompass common business items such as Venn diagrams, which show the intersection of several data sets, and organization charts, which describe the hierarchy of a company or other organization.

Working with Graphics in Your Worksheets

When you add graphics to your worksheets, you go through the Insert tab on the ribbon. The buttons on the Insert tab let you add lines, shapes of many different types, and images to your worksheets. After you create a drawing object, you can change its line color or, if the object has an interior space, you can fill that space with a color or pattern of your choosing. Other ways you can make your images and drawing objects stand out is to add a shadow so the objects appear to float

above the surface of the worksheet. Hard shadows, which you create with black lines, mark the shadowed object as separate from the surrounding items. A softer shadow, one created with a lighter shade of gray, makes the shadowed object appear as part of the collection of objects on the worksheet. You can also add a reflection to an image, adding depth to the image and implying that the worksheet contains a reflective surface.

Adding Graphics to Worksheets

After you've created a worksheet, you can add graphics to enhance the data on the worksheet. If your worksheet details the sales of a specific product, you can add a photograph of the product to the worksheet. Adding a visual representation of the item described in the worksheet makes the results you offer much more memorable. Not only do you and your colleagues have numbers to work with, you also have something solid with which to associate the data, enhancing recall.

See Also

For information on adding a picture to a worksheet header or footer, see "Include a Graphic in a Header or Footer" on page 159.

Add a Picture

1. Click the Insert tab.
2. Click Picture.
3. Navigate to the folder with the picture you want to insert.
4. Double-click the picture you want to insert.

Delete a Picture

1. Click the picture you want to delete.
2. Press the Delete key.

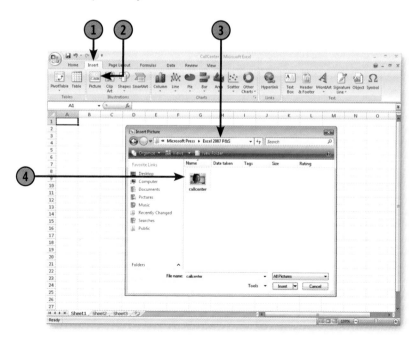

Adding Drawing Objects to a Worksheet

Adding graphics or pictures of items described in your worksheets makes it easier to understand the data in those worksheets; you're not limited to adding images from other sources. If you want, you can add drawing objects to your worksheets. For example, you can add shapes such as rectangles and circles to your worksheets, with the rectangles holding explanatory text and the circles displaying a one- or two-word caption describing the contents of a cell.

Tip

To create a circle or square, instead of an oval or rectangle, hold down the Shift key while you drag the mouse pointer.

Add a Simple Shape

1. Click the Insert tab.

2. In the Illustrations group, click the Shapes button.

3. Click the button representing the shape you want to add.

4. Drag where you want your shape to appear.

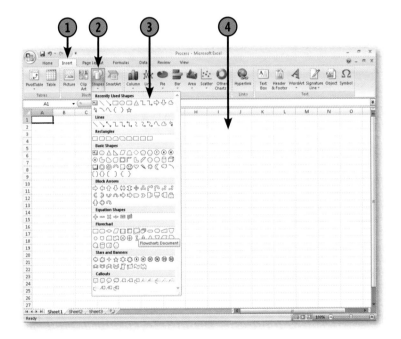

Add Text to Any Shape

1. Click the shape.
2. Type the text you want and press Enter.

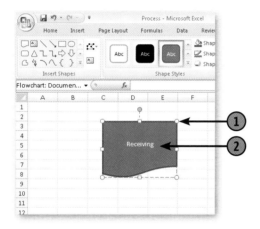

Caution

If the text you add to a shape won't fit in the shape, you'll see only the first part of the text you added. To view the rest of the text, you can enlarge the shape or make the text's font size smaller.

Format Text in a Shape

1. Click the shape.
2. Click the Home tab.
3. Using the controls in the Font group on the ribbon, follow any of these steps:

   - Click the Font down arrow and then click the desired font.
   - Click the Font Size down arrow and then click the desired size.
   - Click the Font Color down arrow and then click the desired color.
   - Use the other controls to assign bold, italic, underline, and other formatting options.

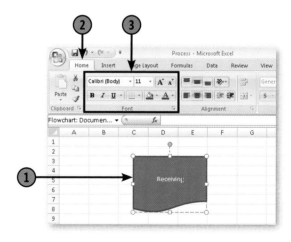

Adding Fills to Drawing Objects

When you create a drawing object in Excel, you create a default version of the object, meaning that the object has the program's usual color or pattern filling its interior. If you want to change the object's appearance, you can select from a series of built-in styles that control the image's fill color, outline, and text color. You can change these colors or patterns to bring the object's appearance in line with your company's color scheme or to make an object stand out from its surroundings.

Apply a Shape Style

1. Click the object you want to format.
2. Click the Format tab.
3. In the Shape Styles group on the ribbon, click the style you want to apply.

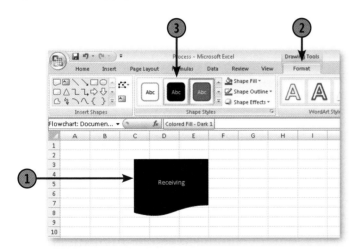

Tip

You can display the entire Shape Styles gallery by clicking the gallery's More button.

Apply a Fill

1. Click the shape you want to fill.
2. Click the Format tab.
3. Click the Shape Fill down arrow and use the controls in the menu that appears to pick a fill color, gradient, or texture.
4. Click the color with which you want to fill the object.

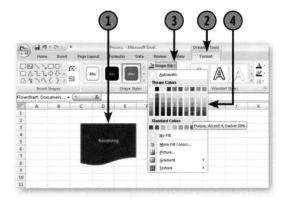

Tip

Textures are a great way to apply a gentle, overall pattern to an object without interfering with any text or image already positioned in the object.

Fill an Object with a Picture

① Click the object you want to fill.

② If necessary, click the Format tab.

③ Click Shape Fill.

④ Click Picture.

⑤ Navigate to where the picture you want is located.

⑥ Double-click the picture you want.

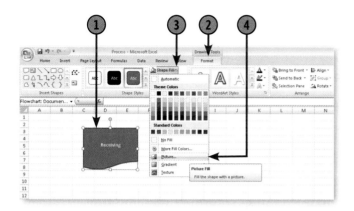

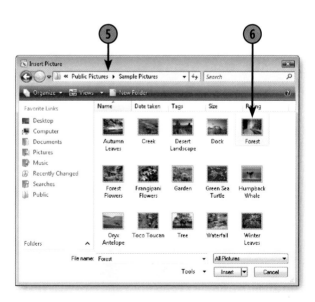

Adding Effects to Drawing Objects

When you add a drawing object to a worksheet, you can add text or color to the object to make it stand out from the rest of the worksheet's contents. Other options you have to make the drawing objects stand out are to add a shadow to the object, which makes it appear that the object is raised off the surface of the worksheet or makes the object appear as if it is three-dimensional. Excel knows how to make its drawing objects appear as three-dimensional objects—all you need to do is describe how you want the object to look!

Add or Edit an Object's Shadow

1 Click the object you want to edit.

2 If necessary, click the Format tab.

3 Click Shape Effects.

4 Click Shadow.

5 Click the shadow style you want for your object.

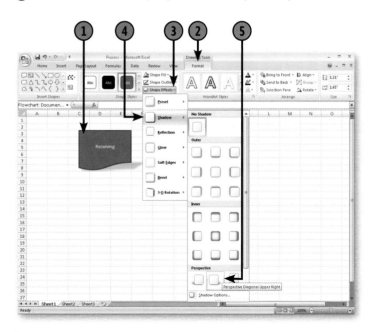

Rotate an Object in Three Dimensions

1 Click the object you want to edit.

2 If necessary, click the Format tab.

3 Click Shape Effects.

4 Click 3-D Rotation.

5 Click the 3-D rotation you want for your object.

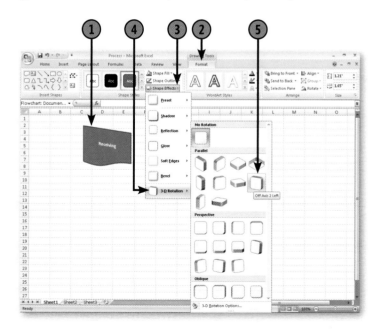

Customizing Pictures and Objects

After you add a picture or drawing object to a worksheet, you can change the object's size to have it take up more or less space on the sheet. You can also rotate the object to change its orientation on the page. Rotating an image a little to one side can imply action or fun, while turning an image upside down indicates something a bit more crazy. Of course, if your image is upside down when you add it to your worksheet, you can rotate it to its "normal" position.

Resize a Picture or Object

① Click the object you want to resize.

② Hover over one of the white handles surrounding the object and drag the handle to the size you want.

Rotate a Picture or Object

① Click the object you want to rotate.

② If necessary, click the Format tab.

③ Follow either of these steps:

   ■ In the Arrange group, click Rotate and then select how you want to rotate the object.

   ■ Hover over the rotation handle (the green dot) and drag the dot to rotate the object to the desired angle.

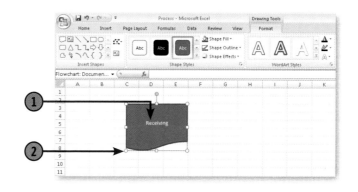

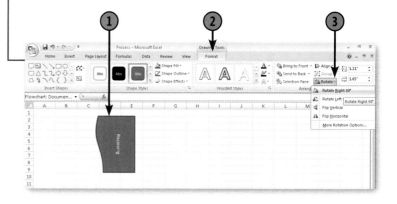

Tip ✔

When you select an object, your object's size dimensions appear in the Size group on the Format tab of the ribbon. If you want to resize your object to a specific size, such as 1.53" wide by 1.77" high, you can type those values directly into the group's fields. You can also click the spin control at the right edge of the field to increase or decrease a dimension by 0.1" per click.

Aligning and Grouping Drawing Objects

One important design element is ensuring any objects that you add to your worksheets are aligned properly, both in relation to the edges of the worksheet and any other objects. If you want a number of your objects to be lined up with each other, such as aligning all objects with the left edge of the page, you can do so. In a similar manner, if you want to work with a set of objects as a single unit, such as three text boxes you want to appear together, regardless of position, you can define the objects as a group and work with them as a single entity.

Align Objects

① Hold down the Ctrl key and click the objects you want to align.

② If necessary, click the Format tab.

③ Click Align.

④ Click how you want to align your objects.

Group or Ungroup Objects

① Hold down the Ctrl key and click the objects you want to group.

② If necessary, click the Format tab.

③ Click the Group button.

④ Click the Group menu item.

Tip

Right-click any object in the group you want to ungroup and click Group, Ungroup. If you have many objects grouped together and ungroup them, you may want to regroup them in the same way. You can do this quickly and easily by right-clicking one of the objects you want to regroup, clicking Group, and clicking Regroup.

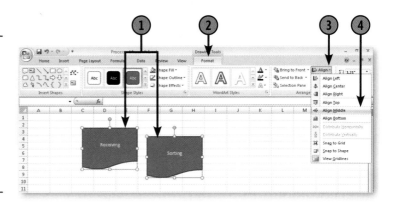

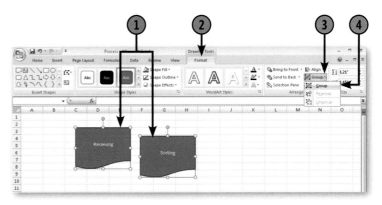

Change the Order of Objects

① Click the object you want to move.

② If necessary, click the Format tab.

③ Follow either of these steps:

■ Click the Bring To Front down arrow and then select whether to bring the object to the front of the stack or to move it up one place.

■ Click the Send To Back down arrow and then select whether to send the object to the back of the stack or to move it back one place.

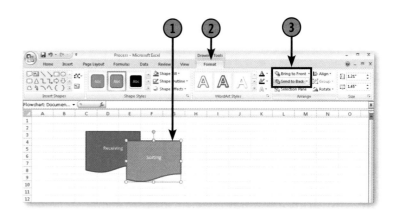

Tip

If you want to apply a format to more than one object, you can group the objects and apply the formatting to all objects at once!

Using WordArt to Create Text Effects in Excel

One of the benefits of working with Microsoft Excel is that you can take advantage of the capabilities of the 2007 Microsoft Office system to enhance your Excel worksheets. One of those capabilities is WordArt, which lets you select from a wide range of styles to add exciting two- and three-dimensional text to your worksheets. Every style comes with a predefined color scheme, but you can change the color, size, and alignment of your WordArt by using the tools on the Home tab of the ribbon.

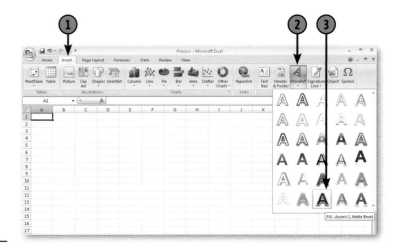

Add WordArt Text

① Click the Insert tab.

② Click WordArt.

③ Click the WordArt style you want.

④ Type the desired text.

⑤ Click the border of the WordArt text.

⑥ Click the Home tab.

⑦ Click the Font down arrow.

⑧ Click the font you want.

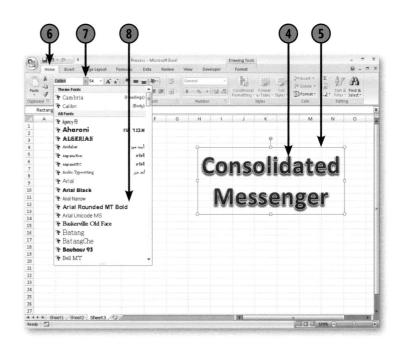

Change WordArt Text Colors

① Click the border of the WordArt you want to format.

② Click the Home tab.

③ Click the Font Color down arrow.

④ Click the desired color.

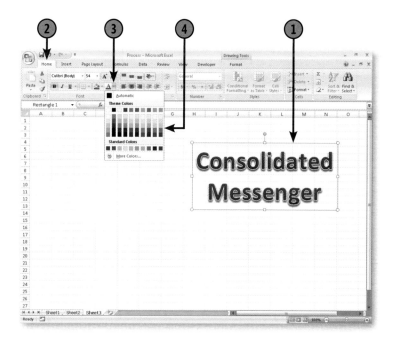

Inserting Clip Art into a Worksheet

If you want to include a worksheet in a presentation you give to your colleagues or for a report you make available on your company's Web site, you can add images from the Clip Art collection that comes with Office to accent your worksheet.

You can manage your clip art by using the Clip Art task pane, whether that means searching for clip art on your computer or on the Web.

Add Clip Art

1. Click the Insert tab.
2. Click Clip Art.
3. Type a description of the Clip Art you want.
4. Click Go.
5. Click the Clip Art you want to insert.

Tip

If you want to find additional clip art, click the Insert tab and then click Clip Art. Then click Clip Art on Office Online in the Clip Art task pane, and you will be directed toward Microsoft's Gallery where you can search from a large number of clips.

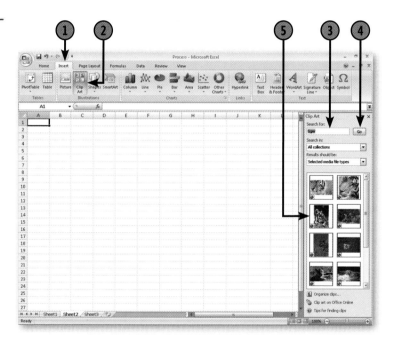

Browse the Clip Organizer for Clip Art

1. Click the Insert tab.

2. Click Clip Art.

3. Click Organize Clips.

4. Click the expand buttons and navigate to the folder that contains the Clip Art you want.

5. Point to the Clip Art you want.

6. Click the down arrow that appears next to the item.

7. Click Paste.

8. Click the Close button.

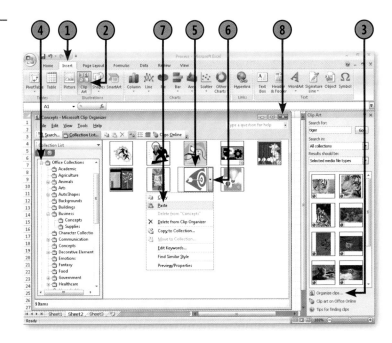

Inserting and Changing a Diagram

A number of diagram types will probably be familiar to most business people: the pyramid, which shows a hierarchical relationship; the target, which uses a ring of concentric circles to display the approach to a target; the Venn diagram, which shows the intersection of items in various sets; and the cycle, which displays the steps in a repeating process. Rather than make you create these diagrams on your own, you can have Excel create the basic diagram and let you fill in the details. After you've created the diagram, you can apply an Auto-Format to alter its appearance.

Insert a Diagram

1. Click the Insert tab.

2. Click SmartArt.

3. Click the category of SmartArt you want to create.

4. Click the specific diagram you want to add to your worksheet.

5. Click OK.

6. Click a text box to add text to your diagram.

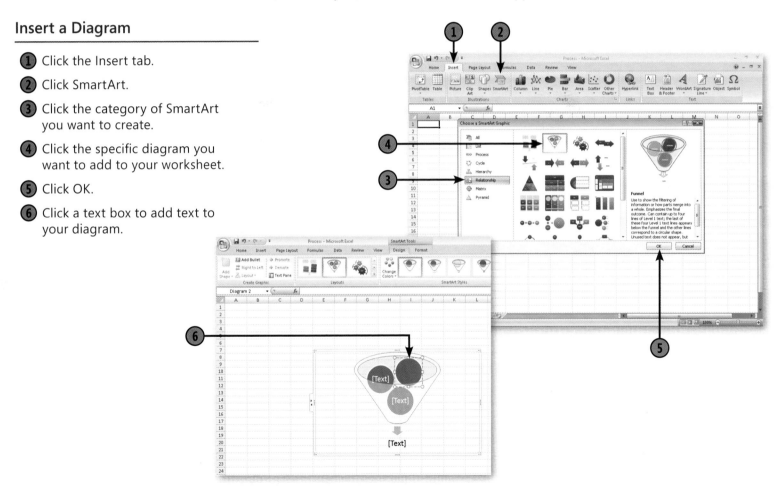

Change the Style of a Diagram

① Click the diagram you want to change.

② Click the Design tab.

③ In the Layouts group on the ribbon, click the layout you want to apply to the diagram.

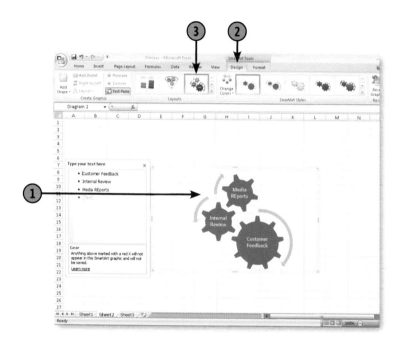

Tip

A preview of the new format appears when you hover the mouse pointer over a layout in the Layouts gallery... feel free to experiment!

Creating an Organization Chart

One of the most important tools in any business is the organization chart, which shows the reporting relationships between employees and their supervisors. Creating the base of an organization chart is simple, as is adding employees to the chart.

After you've created the chart, you can change the chart's direction so the relationships run from left to right and not up and down or apply an AutoFormat to the chart.

Create an Organization Chart

1. Click the Insert tab.
2. Click SmartArt.
3. Click Hierarchy.
4. Click the first graphic in the Hierarchy group.
5. Click OK.

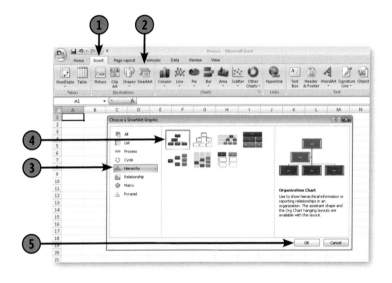

Adding a Shape

1. Click the shape you want to enter a shape under or next to.

2. If necessary, click the Design tab.

3. Click Add Shape.

4. Click the option that reflects where you want to add the shape in the chart.

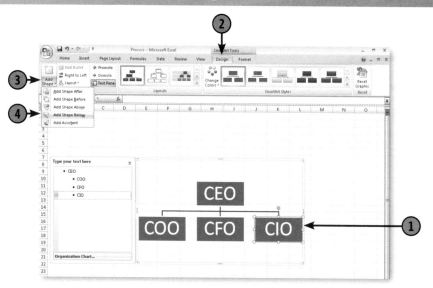

Tip

Click Add Assistant to place the shape below the current shape with an elbow connector.

Alter the Layout of Your Organization Chart

1. Click a shape in the organization chart.

2. Click the Design tab.

3. Click Layout.

4. Click the direction in which you want the shape to extend from the chart.

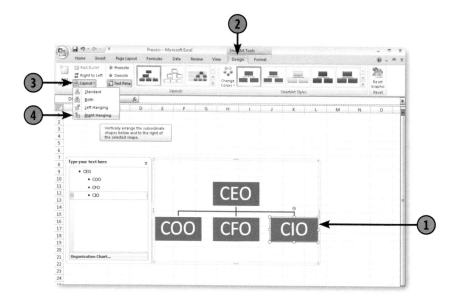

Change the Design of Your Organization Chart

① Click the organization chart you want to change.

② Click the Design tab.

③ Click Change Colors.

④ Click the desired color scheme.

Tip

You can format individual shapes in a SmartArt graphic by clicking the shape you want to format and then clicking the Format tab that appears under SmartArt Tools at the top of the Excel window.

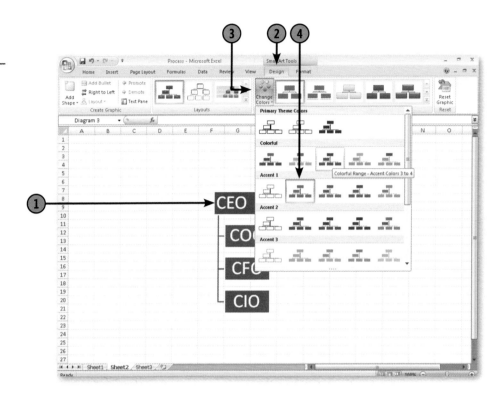

14 Sharing Excel Data with Other Programs

Microsoft Excel 2007 is a powerful program, but it doesn't try to do everything. Other programs in the Microsoft Office 2007 system have complementary strengths: Microsoft Access is ideal for working with large data collections; Microsoft Power-Point lets you create attractive presentations to print or project onto a screen; and Microsoft Word is great for creating text documents. You can include files created in other programs in your Excel workbooks or create links to them. Also, if a colleague uses a database or spreadsheet program that can write its data to a text file, there's a very good chance you can bring that data into Excel.

Introducing Linking and Embedding

Excel works wonderfully as a stand-alone program, but it really shines when you use it in combination with other programs. One way to use Excel in conjunction with other programs is to include in your worksheets files created in other programs, such as graphics, Word documents, or PowerPoint presentations. You can add these objects to your workbooks through linking and embedding.

Keep in mind several important things when you're deciding whether to link to an object or to embed it in a worksheet. As the name implies, embedding an object in a worksheet stores a copy of the object within the workbook. For example, if you wanted to add a company logo to an invoice generated from table data, you can identify the graphic and indicate that you want to embed it in the file. The advantage of embedding an object in an Excel file is that you won't have to worry about the graphic, chart, or image not being available because the person who created the workbook didn't include the graphic.

If you create workbooks with embedded files, you can open your workbook anywhere and be certain your graphics will be available.

A disadvantage of embedding objects in workbooks is that the embedded files can be large and can dramatically increase the size of your workbooks. Although a single, low-resolution logo meant to be viewed on a computer monitor probably won't have much of an impact on your file size, the same image rendered at a resolution suitable for printing might double the size of the workbook. If you embed more than one image, or more than one copy of the same image, you might make your file unworkably large.

When you want to include more than one image or external file in an Excel workbook, you should consider creating a link to the files. For example, rather than embed many copies of a high-resolution logo in your worksheets, you can save the file on your hard disk and link to the file's location on your computer. Excel uses the reference to find the file and display it as part of a workbook. The workbook would be no larger than it was originally, and you wouldn't need to have multiple copies of the same file if you link to it more than once. The advantage of linking is that you save disk space, but the disadvantage is that moving the workbook from computer to computer can be difficult unless you have the extra files when you travel or distribute the workbook to colleagues.

In general, embedding an object in an Excel workbook works best if you only use the object once in the workbook and you have room to store the workbook with the included objects. Otherwise, such as when you use the same file multiple times in the same workbook, you need to link to the file instead.

Linking and Embedding Other Files

Excel workbooks can hold a lot of data, and you can make your data even more meaningful when you include files created with other programs. For example, you might have created a Word document with important background infor- mation or a PowerPoint presentation that puts your data into context for your colleagues. You can include those files in your worksheets by linking or embedding the files as objects.

Embed a File in a Worksheet

1. Click the Insert tab.

2. In the Text group, click Object.

3. Click Create From File.

4. Click Browse.

5. Navigate to the folder that contains the file to which you want to link.

6. Double-click the file you want to embed in your workbook.

7. Click OK.

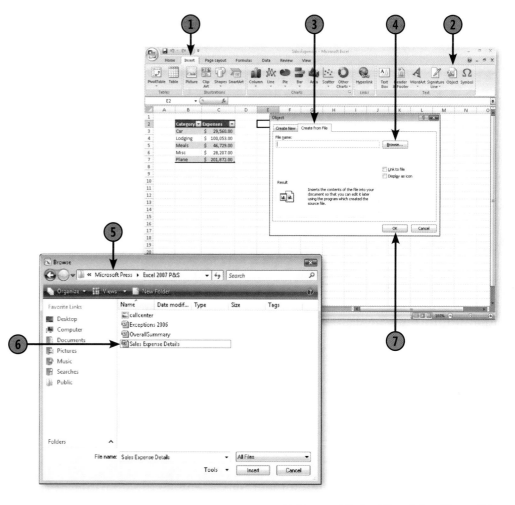

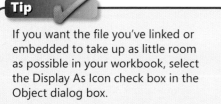

Tip

If you want the file you've linked or embedded to take up as little room as possible in your workbook, select the Display As Icon check box in the Object dialog box.

Link to a File

① Click the Insert tab.

② In the Text group, click Object.

③ Click Create From File.

④ Click Browse.

⑤ Navigate to the folder that contains the file to which you want to link.

⑥ Double-click the file to which you want to link.

⑦ Select the Link To File check box.

⑧ Click OK.

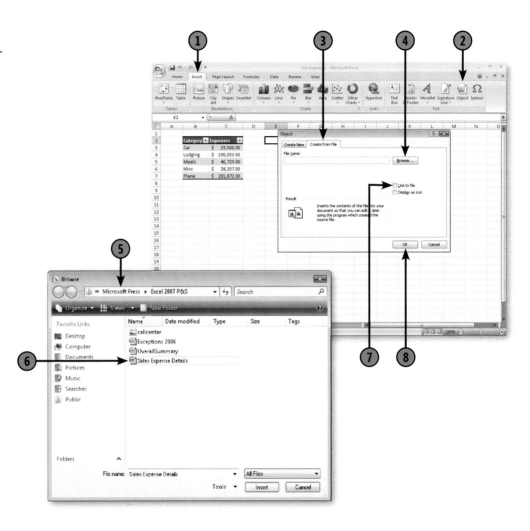

Exchanging Table Data between Excel and Word

Just as you can create workbooks to store and manipulate financial and other data in Excel, you can use Word to create reports and other text documents to interpret and provide valuable context for your worksheet data. Word documents can also present data in tables, which are arranged in rows and columns like a worksheet. For example, if you receive a report from a traveling colleague in which she created a table listing the prices of popular products at a competitor's store, you can copy the data from the Word document to an Excel worksheet for direct comparison. You can also go in the opposite direction, copying Excel data to a table in Word.

Bring Word Data into Excel

① In Word, select the table you want to import into Excel.

② Click the Home tab.

③ Click the Copy button.

④ In Excel, click the cell in which you want the upper left table cell to appear.

⑤ Click the Home tab.

⑥ Click the Paste button.

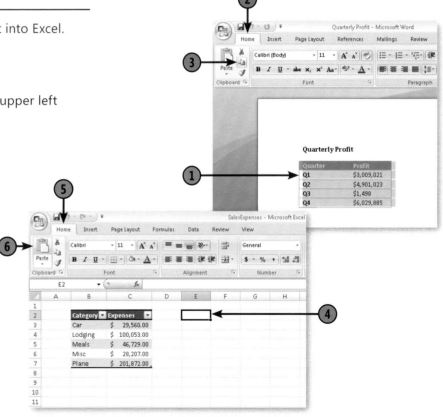

Copy Excel Data to Word

1. In Excel, select the cells you want to export.

2. Click the Home tab.

3. Click the Copy button.

4. In Word, click the location where you want the pasted cells to appear.

5. Click the Home tab.

6. Click the Paste button.

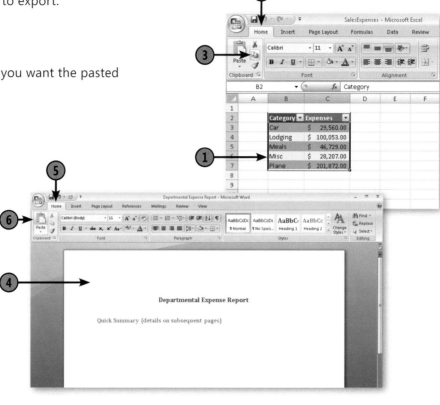

Copying Excel Charts and Data into PowerPoint

It's possible to present Excel data to your colleagues using Excel exclusively, but if you're developing a formal presentation, you might want to use PowerPoint. Because presentations often contain graphic representations of numerical data, it's easy to include your Excel data in a PowerPoint presentation.

When you copy an Excel chart into a PowerPoint presentation, you can select how you want PowerPoint to manage the chart and its data. If you don't make any changes, Power-Point creates the chart and maintains a link to the workbook from which it came. You can also choose to paste the entire workbook into PowerPoint or paste a picture of the chart's current state.

Move Excel Data to PowerPoint

① In Excel, select the cells you want to export.

② Click the Home tab.

③ Click the Copy button.

④ In PowerPoint, click the location where you want the pasted cells to appear.

⑤ Click the Home tab.

⑥ Click the Paste button.

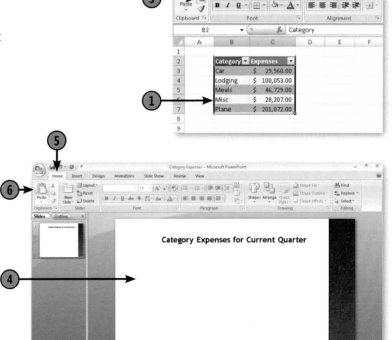

Copy an Excel Chart
to PowerPoint

1 In Excel, select the chart you want to export.

2 Click the Home tab.

3 Click the Copy button.

(continued on the next page)

Tip

When you paste an Excel chart into a PowerPoint presentation, clicking the Paste Options button also enables you to select whether you want the chart to retain its original appearance (that is, its Office theme), or to change its appearance based on the presentation's theme.

Copy an Excel Chart
to PowerPoint (continued)

④ In PowerPoint, click the location where you want the pasted chart to appear.

⑤ Click the Home tab.

⑥ Click the Paste button.

⑦ Click the Paste Options button.

⑧ Follow any of these steps:

■ Click the Chart (Linked To Excel Data) option to paste the chart into the presentation and retain a live link to the source workbook.

■ Click the Excel Chart (Entire Workbook) option to paste the chart and a copy of the workbook to the presentation.

■ Click the Paste As Picture option to paste an image of the chart into the presentation.

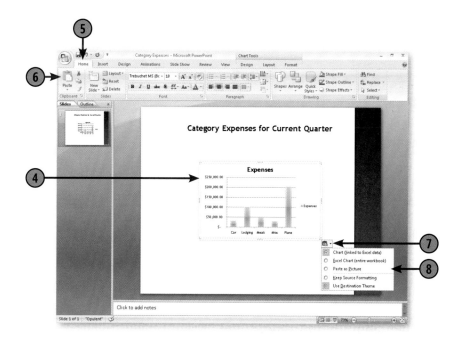

Caution

Neither of the latter two options maintains a live link between the chart and its original workbook. In the first case, you paste a copy of the data into the PowerPoint presentation; in the second, you're just taking a picture of the chart and pasting that into the presentation.

Exchanging Data between Access and Excel

No other Microsoft Office 2007 system programs have as much in common as Access and Excel, but each program has its unique strengths. Where Excel offers a wide range of data analysis and presentation tools you can use to summarize your data, Access is designed to let you store, manipulate, and ask questions of large data collections. You can also use Access queries to locate and summarize table data. Although it is possible to look up data in an Excel worksheet, it's much easier to do in Access.

Bring Access Table Data into an Excel Worksheet

1 In Access, display the table from which you want to copy the data.

2 Select the table cells you want to copy.

3 Click the Home tab.

4 Click Copy.

5 In Excel, click the cell where you want the first table cell to appear.

6 Click the Home tab.

7 Click Paste.

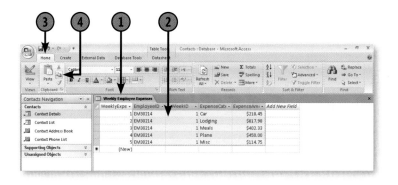

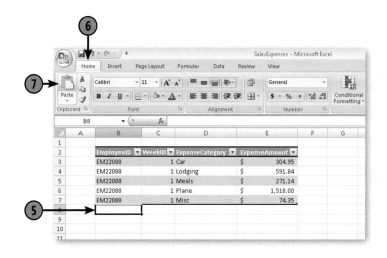

Send Excel Data to Access

① In Excel, select the cells you want to copy.

② Click the Home tab.

③ Click Copy.

④ In Access, display the table that you want to receive the pasted data.

⑤ In the (New) record row, select as many cells as there are columns of data to be pasted.

⑥ Click the Home tab.

⑦ Click Paste.

⑧ Click Yes to acknowledge that you want to paste the worksheet data into the table.

Caution

If you click only a single cell in the Access table's New record row, you'll paste all of your worksheet data into a single table cell, making the table row worthless.

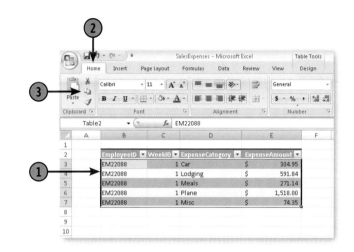

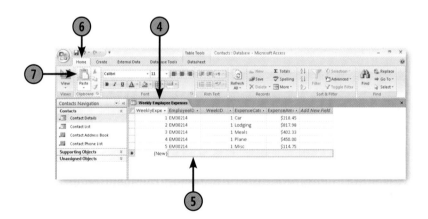

Importing a Text File

Excel can read data from quite a few other spreadsheet and database programs, but you may have a colleague who uses a spreadsheet or database program that creates files you can't read with Excel. If that's the case, you can ask your colleague to save the file as a text file, using a comma, tab, or other char-acter (called a delimiter) to mark the end of each cell's data. Even if you're unable to transfer data any other way, you can always read spreadsheet data if it's presented to you in a text file. Any formatting or formulas will be lost, but the data will be there for you to analyze.

Bring Text into Excel

① Click the Data tab.

② In the Get External Data group, click From Text.

③ Navigate to the folder that contains the text file you want to import.

④ Double-click the text file.

(continued on the next page)

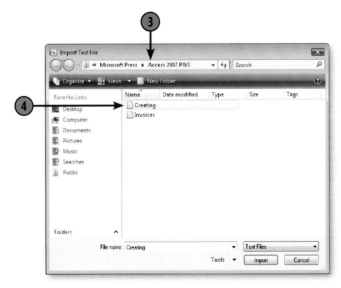

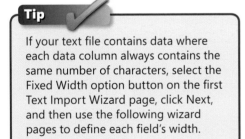

Tip

If your text file contains data where each data column always contains the same number of characters, select the Fixed Width option button on the first Text Import Wizard page, click Next, and then use the following wizard pages to define each field's width.

Bring Text into Excel *(continued)*

⑤ Select the Delimited option button.

⑥ Click Next.

⑦ Select the file's delimiter character.

⑧ Verify that the data appears correctly in the Data Preview pane.

⑨ Click Finish.

⑩ Click OK.

If you can choose whether to have a text file created so that it contains fixed-width or delimited values, ask for the delimited values. Character delimiters are much easier for Excel to detect, which means less work for you when you want to import the data.

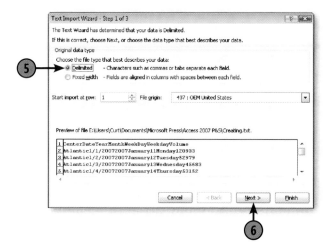

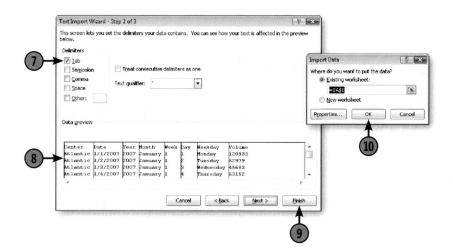

15 Using Excel in a Group Environment

Even though single individuals might be in charge of managing a company's financial data and related information, there is usually a group of folks who either enter data into workbooks or can have input into future revenue or growth projections. You and your colleagues can add comments to workbooks to describe the contents and offer insights into how certain values were derived. If you and your colleagues need to open or edit a workbook at the same time, but from different computers, you can turn on workbook sharing so more than one person can have the workbook open at a time. You can view any changes your colleagues make and then accept or reject those changes to produce a final version of a workbook.

Excel 2007 also takes full advantage of the Extensible Markup Language (XML). XML is a content markup language, meaning that an XML file has information about the data contained within it, not just how the data should be displayed. Not only is the Excel 2007 file format based on XML, you can also save your Excel workbooks as SpreadsheetML (Spreadsheet XML) files, which means your Excel data will be readable by a wide range of programs, not just those programs listed in the Save As dialog box's Save As Type drop-down list.

Sharing Workbooks in Excel

When you want to enable more than one individual to work with a workbook simultaneously, you must turn on workbook sharing. Workbook sharing is perfect for mid-sized businesses in which employees need to look up customer, sales, and product data frequently. In larger companies, turning on workbook sharing makes it possible for co-workers at different offices to add values to a workbook used to develop a cost estimate or maintain expense reports.

Turn on Workbook Sharing

1. Click the Review tab.

2. Click Share Workbook.

3. Select the Allow Changes By More Than One User... check box.

4. Click OK to close the dialog box.

5. Click Save to save the workbook.

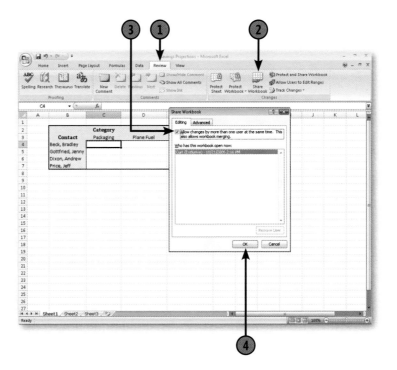

Commenting in Cells

When you and your colleagues share the responsibility for creating a workbook, you might want to add comments to some cells to suggest modifications to a formula, to ask whether a cell's contents might be formatted differently, or to provide an updated value for a workbook's owner to add after they verify the data. Excel 2007 marks cells with comments by placing a red flag at the top right corner, making it easy for you and your colleagues to identify which cells have additional information available. For example, you could add a comment to a sales worksheet explaining that two exceptionally large purchases pushed one hour's sales way beyond the norm.

Add a Comment

① Click the cell to which you want to add a comment.

② Click the Review tab.

③ Click New Comment.

④ Type the comment you want.

⑤ Click anywhere outside the comment to stop adding text.

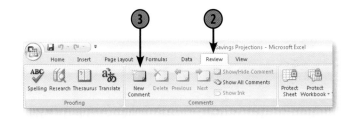

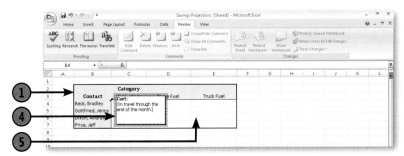

View a Comment

■ Hover over a cell with a red triangle in the upper right corner.

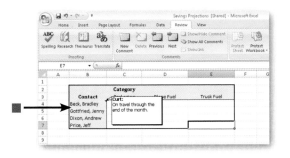

Tip

By default, Excel displays the red flag at the top right corner of only cells that contain comments. If you want a cell's comments to be shown the entire time your workbook is open, right-click the cell with the comment and then click Show/Hide Comments from the shortcut menu. If a cell's comments are shown the entire time, you can return to just the indicator by right-clicking the cell and then clicking Hide Comment.

Edit a Comment

① Select the cell that contains the comment.

② Click the Review tab.

③ Click Edit Comment.

④ Edit the comment text.

⑤ Click anywhere outside the comment box to stop editing.

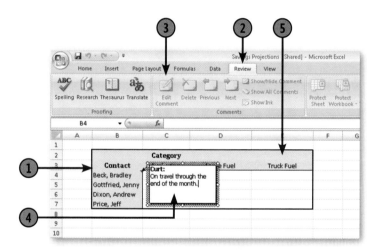

Delete a Comment

① Select the cell that contains the comment.

② Click the Review tab.

③ Click Delete.

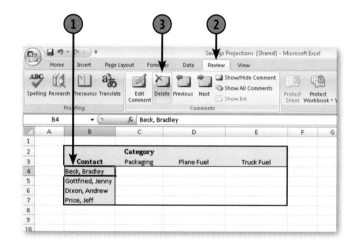

Caution

Note that the name attributed to a comment may not be the same as the person who actually created it. Instead, a comment reflects the name of the person who was logged in to the computer on which the comment was made.

Tracking Changes in Workbooks

Whenever you collaborate with a number of your colleagues in producing or editing a document, you should consider tracking the changes each user makes. When you turn on Track Changes, Excel 2007 highlights any changes made to the workbook in a color assigned to the user who made the changes. When you have a question about a change, you can quickly identify who made it and verify that it is correct.

Turn on Track Changes

① Click the Review tab.

② Click Track Changes.

③ Click Highlight Changes.

④ Select the Track Changes While Editing check box.

⑤ Select the Who check box.

⑥ Click the Who down arrow.

⑦ Click Everyone.

⑧ Click OK.

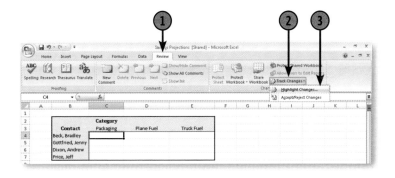

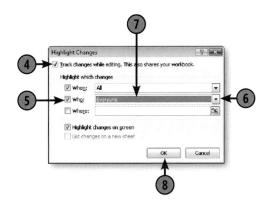

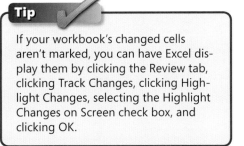

Tip

If your workbook's changed cells aren't marked, you can have Excel display them by clicking the Review tab, clicking Track Changes, clicking Highlight Changes, selecting the Highlight Changes on Screen check box, and clicking OK.

Accepting or Rejecting Changes

When you and your colleagues have made your changes to a workbook, you can go through the workbook and accept or reject those changes. The best way to accept or reject changes is to move through them one at a time. Although examining each change in a large document can be tedious, it's far less of a hassle to take an hour to finalize a workbook than it is to spend a day reconstructing a workbook after you accidentally accepted every change. If you want to keep track of every change, you can have Excel create a new worksheet named History and list every change made since you last saved. Whenever you save your workbook, Excel will delete the History worksheet.

View a Change

- Hover over a cell with a blue triangle in the upper left corner.

Review Changes

① Click the Review tab.

② Click Track Changes.

③ Click Accept/Reject Changes and then click OK to save your workbook.

④ Select the Who check box.

⑤ Click the Who down arrow.

⑥ Click Everyone.

⑦ Click OK.

⑧ Do any of the following:

- Click Accept to accept the current change.
- Click Reject to reject the current change.
- Click Accept All to accept all the changes.
- Click Reject All to reject all the changes.
- Click Close to stop reviewing changes.

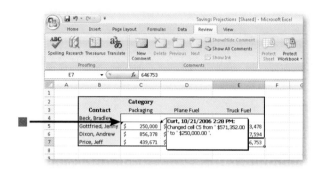

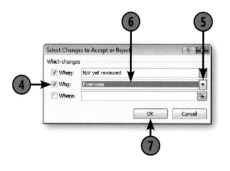

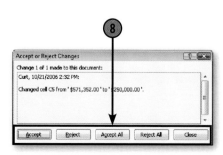

Create a Change History

① Click the Review tab.

② Click Track Changes.

③ Click Highlight Changes.

④ Select the Track Changes While Editing check box.

⑤ Select the Who check box.

⑥ Click the Who down arrow.

⑦ Click Everyone.

⑧ Select the List Changes On A New Sheet check box.

⑨ Click OK.

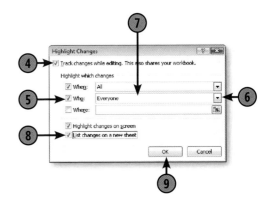

Tip

You should consider making a backup copy of your work-book before accepting any changes. Having a record of what changes were made in case something goes wrong is never a bad idea.

Tip

If you want to review only those changes made after a specific date, click the When down arrow in the Highlight Changes dia-log box, click Since Date, and type the date in the When box.

Saving Worksheets to the Web

Exchanging data with traveling colleagues presents a real challenge to all organizations. Writing the data to a Web page means that you don't have to send the entire workbook to travelers. In fact, your colleagues don't even need Excel on their machines! Saving workbooks as Web pages also enables you to make data available over a corporate network (an *intranet*). So long as your company's network supports Web connections, you can make your data available to any authorized user.

Save a Workbook to the Web

1. Click the Microsoft Office button.

2. Click Save As.

3. Click the Save As Type down arrow.

4. Click Web Page.

5. Navigate to the folder where you want to save your workbook.

6. Type the file name you want.

7. Click Save.

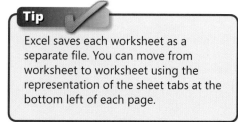

Tip

Excel saves each worksheet as a separate file. You can move from worksheet to worksheet using the representation of the sheet tabs at the bottom left of each page.

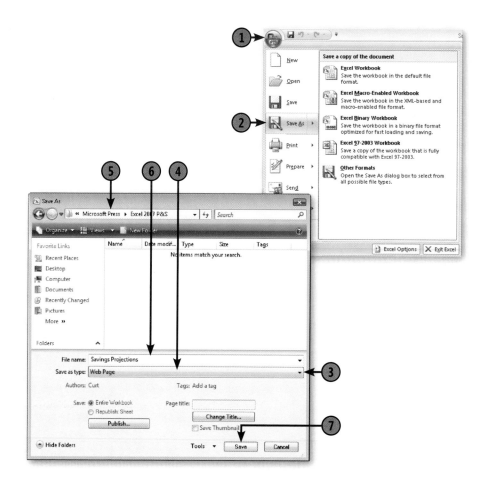

Add a Worksheet to an Existing Web Page

① Display the worksheet you want to add to an existing Web page.

② Click the Microsoft Office button.

③ Click Save As.

④ Click the Save As Type down arrow.

⑤ Click Web Page.

⑥ Select the Selection: Sheet option.

⑦ Verify that the name of the file to which you want to add the worksheet appears in the File Name box.

⑧ Click Save.

⑨ In the message box that appears, click Add To File.

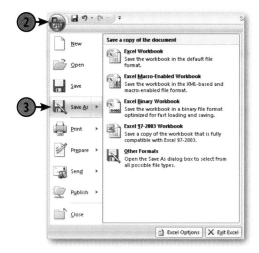

Tip

You can change the text that appears on the title bar of the Excel document's Web page by clicking the Change Title button in the Save As dialog box.

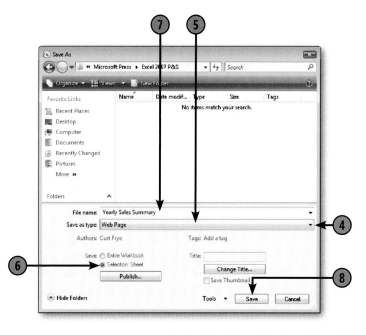

Dynamically Update Worksheets Published to the Web

One advantage of working with Excel over the Web is that you can make it possible for you and your colleagues to interact with Excel worksheets you have published on the Web. By adding interactivity to your worksheet, you and your colleagues can edit cell values, sort the values in the worksheet, filter, or create formulas. You can also use interactivity to update an Excel-based Web page whenever there is a change in the workbook on which the file is based.

Dynamically Update Worksheets Published to the Web

1. Click the Microsoft Office button.
2. Click Save As.
3. Click the Save As Type down arrow.
4. Click Web Page.
5. Click Publish.
6. Click the Choose down arrow.
7. Click the sheet that contains the data you want to update.
8. Select the AutoRepublish Every Time This Workbook Is Saved check box.
9. Click Publish.

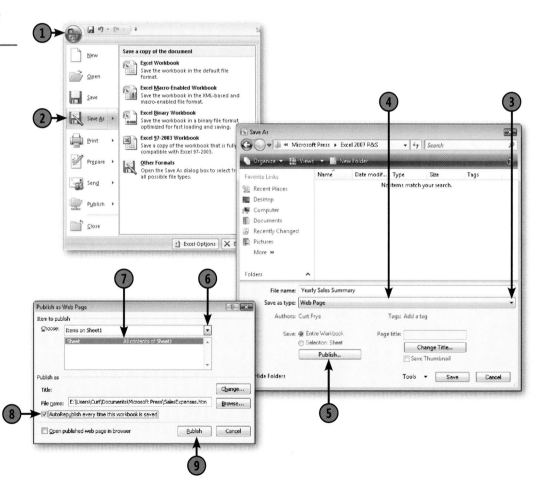

Retrieving Web Data from Excel

The World Wide Web is a great source of information. From stock quotes to product descriptions, many companies publish useful information on their Web sites. The most common structure used to present financial information is the table, which, like a spreadsheet, organizes the data into rows and columns. Excel 2007 makes creating a Web query easy by letting you copy data directly from a Web page into Excel and then create a query to retrieve data from the table you copied.

Retrieve Data from Web Pages

1. Click the Data tab.
2. Click From Web.
3. Type the address of the Web page you want.
4. Click Go.
5. Click the yellow boxes with black arrows to specify which tables you want to import.
6. Click Import.
7. Click OK.

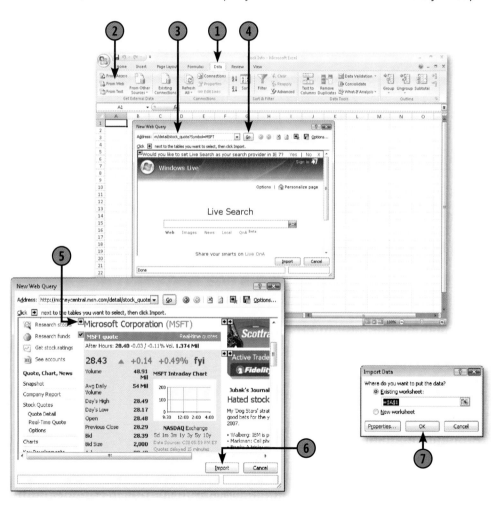

Copy Data from
the Web to Excel

1 In your Web browser, type the URL you want to visit.

2 Select the data you want to copy into Excel.

3 Press Ctrl+C to copy the data to the Clipboard.

4 In Microsoft Excel, click the cell where you want to paste the data.

5 Click the Home tab.

6 Click the Paste button.

Tip

When you paste data from the Web into Excel, you can click the Paste Options button to display a list of options. The last option is Create Refreshable Web Query, which displays the New Web Query dialog box.

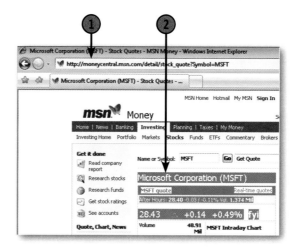

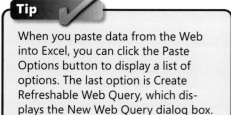

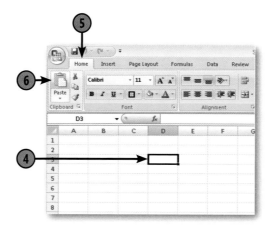

Modifying Web Queries

When you create a Web query, you make it possible to use data from tables on your company's intranet or the Internet in your worksheets. Financial data can change, though, so you should use the buttons on the Data tab of the ribbon to change how Excel deals with data drawn from other sources. One way you can ensure that the external data is current is to have Excel refresh the data regularly.

Schedule Web Query Data Refreshes

① Click the Data tab.

② Click any cell that contains query data.

③ Click the Properties button in the Connections group.

④ Select the Refresh Every check box.

⑤ Type the number of minutes between refreshes in the Minutes box.

⑥ Click OK.

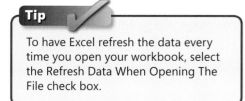

Tip

To have Excel refresh the data every time you open your workbook, select the Refresh Data When Opening The File check box.

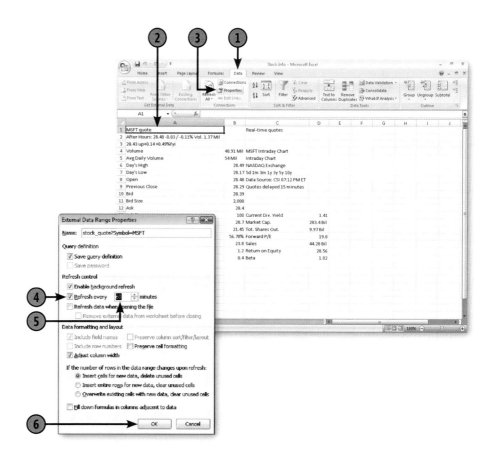

Introducing XML

Although the Hypertext Markup Language (HTML) is great for describing how a Web page should be displayed in a browser, the language isn't designed to communicate anything about the contents of a document. For example, telling Internet Explorer to display a worksheet as an HTML table tells you nothing about the data shown on a Web page. When you save your worksheet data to an XML document, however, Excel annotates the data with tags describing which program generated the data, the name of the worksheet, and the data that belongs in each cell. With that information, Excel, or another spreadsheet program that understands XML data, can read in your worksheet data and retain your original meaning.

Although a full discussion of XML is beyond the scope of this book, the following bit of XML code shows how to identify an Excel workbook in XML:

```
<?xml version="1.0"?>
<Workbook xmlns="urn:schemas-microsoft-com:office:
spreadsheet"  xmlns:o="urn:schemas-microsoft-com:
office:office" xmlns:x="urn:schemas-microsoft-com:
office:excel" xmlns:ss="urn:schemas-microsoft-
com:office:spreadsheet" xmlns:html="http://www.
w3.org/TR/REC-html40">
```

Also, XML can identify rows and cells within the spreadsheet, as in the following example:

```
<Row>
    <Cell><Data ss:
Type="String">Atlantic</Data></Cell>
    <Cell><Data ss:Type="Date">1/1/2007</Data></Cell>
    <Cell><Data ss:Type="Number">2007</Data></Cell>
    <Cell><Data ss:
Type="String">January</Data></Cell>
    <Cell><Data ss:Type="Number">1</Data></Cell>
    <Cell><Data ss:Type="Number">1</Data></Cell>
    <Cell><Data ss:
Type="String">Monday</Data></Cell>
    <Cell><Data ss:
Type="Number">120933</Data></Cell>
</Row>
```

This XML code fragment represents the highlighted row in the following worksheet.

Center	Date	Year	Month	Week	Day	Weekday	Volume
Atlantic	1/1/2007	2007	January		1	1 Monday	120933
Atlantic	1/2/2007	2007	January		1	2 Tuesday	52979

Interacting over the Web with XML

The goal of XML is to be a universal language, allowing data to move freely from one application to another. In this case, that means that saving an Excel worksheet as an XML document would allow any other spreadsheet program to read the XML

file, separate out the cell names and data, and use the annotations to recreate the worksheet. By the same token, you could take a worksheet saved as an XML file and, regardless of the program in which the file was created, import it into Excel.

Save a Workbook as an XML Spreadsheet

1 Click the Microsoft Office button.

2 Click Save As.

3 Click the Save As Type down arrow.

4 Click XML Spreadsheet 2003.

5 Type the file name you want.

6 Click Save.

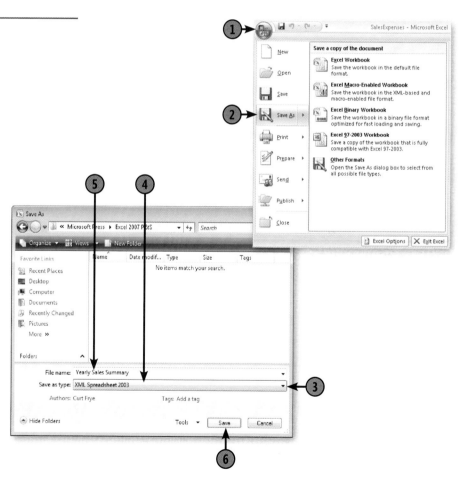

Import Spreadsheet XML

1. Click the Microsoft Office button.

2. Click Open.

3. Navigate to the folder containing the XML document you want.

4. Double-click the XML document.

Tip

If you don't see any XML documents in the Open dialog box, click the file type button and click All Microsoft Excel Files.

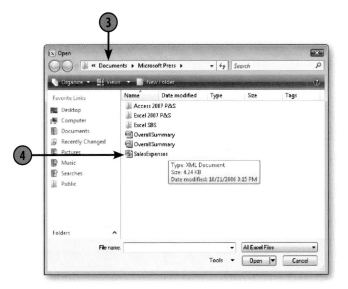

Index

J

jargon, 1–2

K

keyboard shortcuts, 33
Keywords field, 19

L

landscape mode, 143, 154
layout, charts, 198
Left Arrow key, 33
legends, charts, 200
library, function, 93
line breaks, 35
line chart, 196
linking files, 234–36
links, formulas, 87–88
locking cells, 142

M

mailto: hyperlinks, 49
margins, print, 152–53
Maximize button, 23
meeting conditions, 119
menus. *See* ribbon
merging cells, 124
Microsoft Office Assistance Center site, 30
Microsoft Office button, 6
Minimize button, 23
Mini toolbar, 7, 72, 100
moving worksheets, 59–60
multi-column sorts, 181
multiple pages, printing, 155
multiple workbooks, 22, 75

N

Name box, 14
Name Manager, 83
named ranges, 82–84, 96
New Book option, 61
new features, 5–12
    chart creation, 12
    color management, 10
    conditional formats, 11
    data tables, 7
    Dialog Expander, 6
    formatting capabilities, 5
    functions, 9
    galleries, 7
    Microsoft Office button, 6
    Mini toolbar, 7
    ribbon, 5–6
    rules, 11
    themes, 10
    user interface, 5–6
no Borders option, 51
number formats, 6
Number group (Home tab), 6
numbers, cell entry, 36
numerical data, formatting, 102–03

O

Object dialog, 235
objects, formatting, 7
Open dialog box, 26
opening workbooks, 17
order of conditions, formatting, 120
order of objects, 223
organization charts, 230–32
    Add Assistant, 231
    creating, 230
    design, 232

organization charts, *continued*
    layout, 231
    shapes, adding, 231
orientation, printing, 154
outlining, 138–39

P

page breaks, 161–62
Page Down key, 33
Page Layout tab (ribbon), 6, 128
Page Layout View, 144–45
Page Setup dialog, 155
Page Up key, 33
paper, choosing, 149
Paste option, 51
Paste as Hyperlink option, 51
Paste Link option, 51
Paste as Picture option, 51
Paste as Picture Link option, 51
Paste Special option, 51
Paste Values option, 51
pasting cell values, 51
patterns
    formatting, 106
    objects, 218
Percent Style button, 102
Pick from Drop-Down List items, 40
pictures, 215, 219. *See also* graphics
pie chart, 196, 208–10
    3-D exploded, 209
    3-D options, 210
    slicing, pulling out, 208
portrait mode, 143, 154
positioning worksheets, 60
PowerPoint, data sharing, 239–41
precedents, formulas, 96
previewing, 144–45, 153, 155
print areas, 150

splitting worksheets, 74
Start button, 16
Start menu, 16
starting program, 16
Status bar, 14
stock charts, 196, 211
Stop If True, 119
styles
    applying, 109
    charts, 198
    creating, 110
    defined, 109
    deleting, 112
    modifying, 111
Styles group (Home tab), 6
subtotals, 91–92
SUMIF function, 9
SUMIFS function, 9
summary formulas, 89–92
surface chart, 196
Switch Windows, 22
symbols, 45
Symbol tab, 45

T

Tab Color options, 64
Tab key, 33
table columns, selecting, 43
table references, formulas, 85
Table Tools, 42
tables, 7
templates, 164–67
    modifying, 166
    online, 165
    workbooks, creating from, 164–65
    workbooks, saving as, 167
text
    alignment, 113

text, *continued*
    appearance, 101
    cell entries, 35
    colors, 225
    effects, 224–25
    finding, 54
    graphics, 217
    orientation, 114
    replacing, 55
    wrapping, 113–14
text files, importing, 244–45
Text Import Wizard, 244
text value, numbers, 36
textures, 218
themes, 10, 60, 126–28
    applying, 126
    colors, changing, 126
    creating, 128
    effects, changing, 127
    fonts, changing, 127
times, entering, 37–38
Title Bar, 14, 23
titles, charts, 201
toolbars. *See* ribbon
totals, 91
Trace Dependents button, 96
Trace Precedents button, 96
tracer arrows, 96
Track Changes, 251
Transpose option, 51
trendlines, charts, 212
Try This! exercises
    AutoFill data entry, 39
    commonly used formulas, 81
    conditional formatting, 116
    data tables, header rows, 42
    printing, Fit To option, 155
    text entry in cells, 35
types, charts, 196, 199

U

Undo button, 54
Ungroup Sheets option, 72
ungrouping graphics, 222
Unhide command, 63
unhiding worksheets, 63
unique values, 192
Up Arrow key, 33
user interface, 5–6, 15

V

validating data, 188–90
value axis scale, charts, 203
value series. *See* AutoFill
values
    duplicate, 193
    unique, 192
vertical scroll bars, 14
View tab (ribbon), 6, 22, 77–78
viewing worksheets, 58, 74–75
views, worksheets, 77–78

W

watches, formulas, 98
Web, saving to, 254
Web data, retrieving, 257–58
Web queries, 259
Web pages
    data, copying, 258
    data, retrieving, 257
    hyperlinks, 48
    updating, 256
    workbooks, adding, 255
windows
    resizing, 23

X–Y

Z

About the Author

Curt Frye is a freelance writer and Microsoft Office Excel Most Valuable Professional from Portland, Oregon. He is the author of *Microsoft Office Excel 2007 Step By Step, Microsoft Office Excel 2007 Plain & Simple, Microsoft Office Access 2007 Plain & Simple,* and numerous articles for the Microsoft Office Work Essentials Web site.